D1547047

A Time in Turkey

A Time in Turkey

Craig Mair

JOHN MURRAY

TRANSATLANTIC ARTS, INC.
Levittown, New York 11756
SOLE DISTRIBUTOR FOR THE U.S.A.

Printed in Great Britain by
The Camelot Press Ltd,
London & Southampton

0 7195 2836 4

To my parents
Trudie and George

Contents

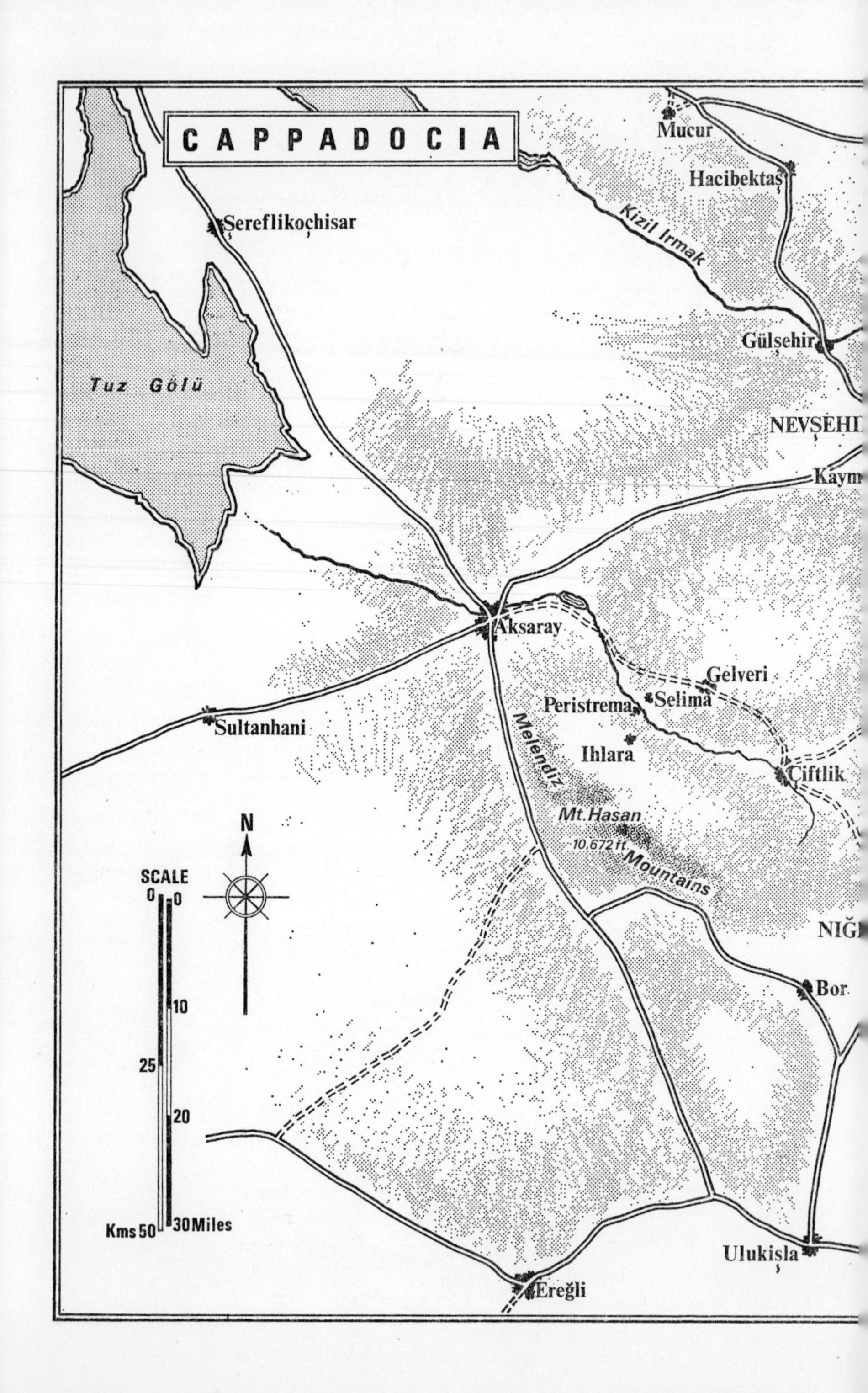
CAPPADOCIA
Mucur
Hacibektaş
Şereflikoçhisar
Kizil Irmak
Gülşehir
Tuz Gölü
NEVŞEHI
Kaym
Aksaray
Gelveri
Peristrema
Selima
Sultanhani
Melendiz
Ihlara
Çiftlik
N
Mt.Hasan
10.672 ft.
Mountains
SCALE
0
0
10
25
20
Kms 50
30 Miles
NIĞ
Bor
Ulukişla
Ereğli

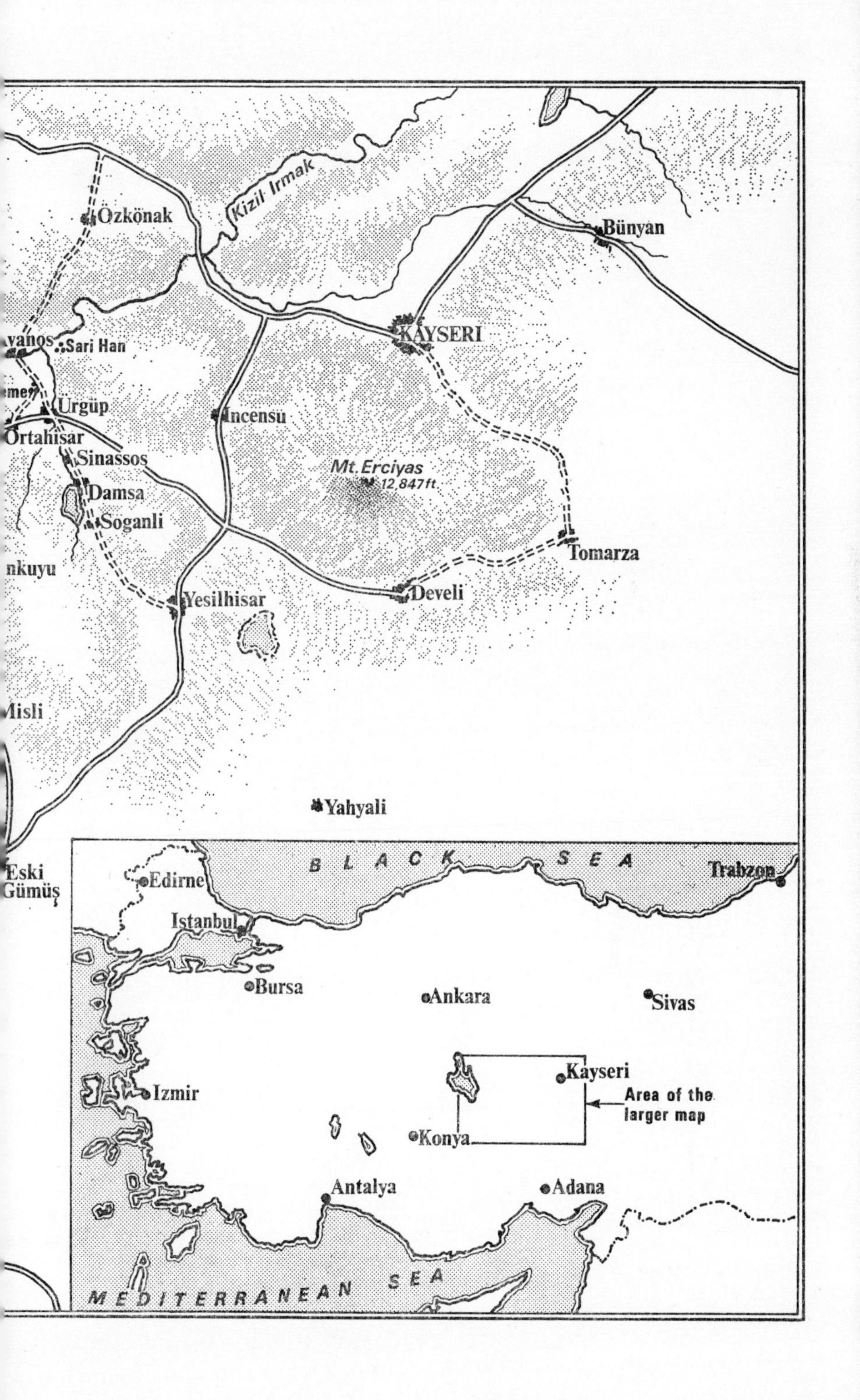

Kizil Irmak
Özkönak
Bünyan
KAYSERI
Sari Han
Ürgüp
Incensu
Ortahisar
Sinassos
Mt. Erciyas
12,847 ft.
Damsa
Soganli
Tomarza
Yesilhisar
Develi
Yahyali
Eski
Gümüş
BLACK SEA
Edirne
Trabzon
Istanbul
Bursa
Ankara
Sivas
Kayseri
Izmir
Area of the larger map
Konya
Antalya
Adana
MEDITERRANEAN SEA

Illustrations

From the author's photographs

Illustrations

Author's Note

One difficulty in writing this book has been in the spelling of Turkish place names. Some villages still call themselves by their old Greek names, originally used when they were still Orthodox Christian communities, even though they now have official Turkish alternatives which are used on maps and documents. I have therefore employed the names used by the villagers themselves, though where reasonably common alternatives exist, these have sometimes been added in brackets. Occasionally I have added translations of interesting place names.

Some readers may also have difficulties with Turkish spelling, but it is in fact really very easy. Turkish is a phonetic language, spoken exactly as it is written, but pronouncing every letter—it is therefore only necessary to learn how each letter is pronounced. The only exceptions to the English pronunciation of letters are the following: 'c' = English 'j' as in *jam-jar*; 'ç' = English 'ch' as in *church*; 'ğ' simply lengthens the previous vowel as in *oğlu*= *awloo*; 'ı' is not important; 'j' = English soft 'j' as in French '*je* suis'; 'ö' = German 'ö'; 'ş' = English 'sh' as in *ship*; 'ü' = German 'ü'. Examples for learning might include *çurç*, *cam-car*, *şip*, and *doktor*. Two exceptions are the words *paşa* and *şiş kebap*, which I have generally rewritten as *pasha* and *shish kebap*, because the words have now become so Anglicised.

I would also like to acknowledge, with sincere thanks, the following people and organisations, who in many different ways helped me during my stay in Turkey, or in writing this book: Mr John Sanson, whose Award from George Watson's College in Edinburgh made the entire trip possible; Mr Roger Young and Mr Alex Gibson in Edinburgh; Mr Rüknettin Ülütüg and Mr Doktoroğlu in Istanbul; Mehmet Ali and friends at the Bazaar; Mr Yaşar Güven, the Köse family, and Tahir; Bayram Boylu, Hasan Kiran, and many many more friends in Ortahisar; the entire Algan family in Istanbul; the assistants in several dual-national libraries and institutes at Ankara and Istanbul; the librarians in Ürgüp and Ortahisar; Sir Steven Runciman for the use of his library; and finally my parents, my brother, my wife Anne, and Mrs Osyth Leeston, for their help with this manuscript. To all these people I extend gratitude and thanks.

Upper Kinneil House A.C.M.
Old Polmont
Stirlingshire

Glossary

The following list of words may be found useful in the understanding of this book:

anne: mother.
ayran: watered yogurt.
baba: father.
bayram: festival or holiday.
bey: mister (John Smith would be either John *bey* or John Smith *bey* but not *bey* Smith).
börek: pie or pastry. There are many varieties of this favourite Turkish food, both savoury or meaty, rolled or flaky.
cami: mosque.
ciborium: In this sense, the small minaret found on the roofs of many Cappadocian mosques—unique in the entire Islamic world to this one area.
dağ: mountain (plural: *dağlari*) e.g. Hasan dağ, Melendiz dağlari.
dolmuş: A communal taxi which generally has no fixed route, but which lifts and deposits passengers wherever they want to go, so long as the destination of any one passenger fits in with all the others.
eski: old or ancient, e.g. Eski Gümüş means 'Old Silver'.
hammam: Turkish bath.
han: A caravanserai; a fortified stopping place used by trading caravans throughout the East, usually spaced a day's journey apart.
hisar: A castle or fortress, e.g. *Yeşil Hisar* means 'Green Castle' and *Ortahisar* means 'Middle Castle'.
hoca: The teacher, or sometimes priest, in a mosque.
kale: Tower, fortress, or castle.
kara: black.
karanlık: dark or darkened.
kebap: meat roasted over charcoal—a very general term.
kilise: Church or chapel.
kızıl: red, e.g. *Kızılırmak* means the 'Red River'.
köfte: rissoles or meatballs, often cooked over charcoal.

Glossary

köy: village.

lokanta: A restaurant where food is served.

lokantası: A restaurant where only refreshments are served.

lokum: Turkish Delight.

medresse: An Islamic seminary or religious school.

millet: Nation or people, e.g. *Türk Millet* means the Republic of Turkey.

mihrab: The steep, stepped pulpit in a mosque.

muezzin: The man who calls the Faithful to prayer five times daily in all Mohammedan countries.

oğlu: son or son of, the equivalent of 'Mac' to a Scotsman perhaps.

orta: middle or centre, e.g. *Ortahisar*, or *orta şekerli kahve*, which means 'middle sweet coffee' (Turkish coffee is made with the sugar already in it, so you have to say what kind you prefer when ordering).

pilav: rice.

raki: An aniseed alcoholic drink similar to Pernod, and which turns from clear to milky when water is added.

saray: palace, mansion, or government house.

şiş: skewer, e.g. *shish kebap* is meat roasted on a skewer over charcoal.

yeni: new.

1 *First Steps in Turkey*

People go to Turkey for many different reasons. Some like to potter about amongst Anatolia's wealth of archaeological remains, or to swim in warm blue waters, sheltered by secret coves. Others enjoy photographing colourful peasants or magnificent mosques, or perhaps hope to seek out the belly dancers of Stamboul. I went for quite a different reason.

My father, who is a doctor, had for some years been a regular visitor to Turkey. On his first trip he had discovered the village of Ortahisar where, lost in central Anatolia, he found that there was no doctor, but a desperate local need for one. Something must have roused his compassion and medical skill, for he stayed on in the village, running a busy surgery in the local restaurant until his medical supplies were exhausted. On subsequent trips he took extra medicines with him for the benefit of this picturesque, dusty village. I think that he was the only doctor the villagers had ever known—certainly the people always waited for his return. When I arrived I found my father's portrait hanging everywhere; displayed with pride and affection in all those little homes.

I had heard so much from my father about Turkey and especially the village of Ortahisar that I longed to go there. My chance came when I was eighteen and received an Award of £250 given to promote initiative, self-reliance and independence and it was arranged that I should spend a pre-university year living in Turkey. My father, who had not been back for three or four years, was delighted to be able to send me as a sort of 'gift' to the village. Ortahisar's head man wrote assuring us that medical, educational and general odd-job aid were all much needed.

Although at that time I knew no Turkish, I hoped that my knowledge of French, German and Dutch would help when English was not understood. Also I hoped soon to become fluent in Turkish by living in Turkish households. I had recently completed several First Aid courses which, linked to my medical home environment, would, I decided be enough to give simple treatment to the sick in Ortahisar. My father felt that in rural Turkey most illnesses would be straightforward, neither caused nor complicated by stress factors. I studied the uses of several medicaments and pills, and then my father and I packed a large brown suitcase full of bottles, ointments, tubes, bandages, thermometers, plasters, dressings and splints. I took no syringes, however, for that would have been beyond my brief. Amongst my other luggage I took my guitar, camera and my typewriter.

Many people still travel to Istanbul in the hope of finding the gateway to the East, the meeting place of their way of life and ours. The only way to find anything at all is to stay in one place long enough to scratch below the Western veneer and find what lies beneath. But in this age of hurried, crowded itineraries, few travellers have the time to do this. Moreover, few foreigners ever gain deep-rooted local confidence and friendship—another essential prerequisite to finding the genuine old East.

By living in Turkey, I got a different view of things. I was able to scratch through the West's veneer into several contrasting types of Turkish society. Indeed, as I learned Turkish, I almost began to feel Turkish myself, and for a time I found myself adopting Turkish attitudes, even to women and religion. I believe that I really did become integrated into the Turkish way of life in many respects, fully accepted by the people with whom I lived.

27th August

To keep an eye on a trunk, five suitcases, a guitar, and a camera, while disembarking from any train involves a certain amount of physical effort and patience; to attempt to do so while clambering out of the Orient Express is, however, suicidal. So while hundreds of heads bobbed and thronged, shouted and wept, snatched at billowing veils and staggered under impossible loads, I stayed in my compartment and watched, bewildered and amazed. At least I had reached Istanbul, and for the time being it was enough.

Suddenly I saw a couple of heads among the welcoming crowds, bobbing higher and more excitedly than the rest, and waving the familiar photographs which I had posted a few days previously. I smiled, and realised what my father had meant when he said that the Turks never do anything until the last minute: Mehmet Ali may not have acknowledged my letters, but here he was at the station to meet me. Happily I surged out of the train and headed for the bobbing heads with the photos. Then a cry went up behind me, and I discovered to my amazement that we had passed each other in the incredible crowd which swarmed around the platform—Mehmet Ali was already fighting his way towards the exit with a trolley stacked with my baggage.

A customs officer scribbled in my passport and pushed me on, and still gesticulating, we all found ourselves pushed by the crowd into the street. Before I quite knew what was happening I was in a large car, and listening to Mehmet Ali babbling away happily in a language which I did not understand. I was vaguely aware of our car swerving constantly through frightening traffic, and of the fact that the driver played tunes on his horn . . . he had fixed it so that it would perform 'Colonel Bogey'. Minarets flitted past, and I had flashing impressions of colour and crowds, then suddenly we stopped outside a hotel with a sign which said 'Lale Oteli'. My baggage was stacked up into a mountain on the pavement, Mehmet Ali happily pumped my hand, and as quickly as he had materialised, he disappeared again, leaving me alone outside the hotel wondering what had happened.

A boy took my things into the hallway, an oily character showed me to a room, the baggage followed soon after, and it appeared that I was to spend my first night in Istanbul at the 'Lale Oteli'. The oily proprietor said, 'Very nice room, oui? *Ja sehr schön, sehr schön!*' and disappeared. Wearily I sat down on the bed and sadly noted that it was hard.

The room was very small, but it had at least a window which looked out on to the street three floors below. Eagerly I scanned the world which was to be mine for the next year . . . but all that I could see were tiled roofs, strings of washing hanging in the sun, a few minarets jutting up from behind Istanbul's incredible sky-line, and a beggar sitting in the shade of a tree down the street. But it was different, and it was exciting.

It was only then that I saw the cockroach . . . quite the biggest cockroach that I had ever seen. It seemed to saunter quite happily across my bed, then suddenly scurried off, presumably among the sheets and blankets. Then I saw several more of the horrible insects, and the more I looked the more cockroaches I discovered . . . under the bed, crawling in the basin, perched squat and ugly on the very soap with which I was to wash my hands, creeping even under the pillow. Suddenly I felt sick, and with a growing unhappiness replacing my initial exuberance and excitement, I hurriedly left the room and went down to the street to do some exploring.

I had not walked far when I met Mehmet Ali returning to the hotel, still chattering away in Turkish—a language which I found completely unintelligible despite three days with a *Teach Yourself Turkish* book while on the train. Mehmet Ali led me by the arm into a main street, where, among the street sellers and urchins, I gathered we were heading for the Bazaar, for my new-found friend kept pointing towards a cluster of buildings further up the road and saying Bazaar. I was all for visiting the Bazaar, even though I had not yet washed after three and a half days on the Orient Express. But I hardly relished the method by which Mehmet Ali led me there, for in order to reach the Bazaar it was necessary to cross the main street on which we were walking, which seemed a physical impossibility. However, Mehmet Ali suddenly dived into the crowds and in a flash was laughing and hailing me from the other side of the street.

It is written in the brochures which school-children receive about Istanbul, before they disembark from their cruise ships, that 'the traffic in Istanbul drives on the right . . . it also drives on the left, and in the middle!' Let me confirm this immediately, for I was left in no doubt of it by the time I finally made the far side of that main street! There were supposed to be six lanes of traffic . . . there were, in fact, eight. Drivers swerved and hooted, cursed and screeched, in a cacophony of sound which seemed only to increase in venom as soon as I ventured from the pavement. And all the time Mehmet Ali stood on the far side, guffawing at my distress signals. Then he vanished again, and just as I was beginning to think that he had given up waiting for me, he reappeared at my side, took my elbow, and skilfully whisked me between the lanes of snarling traffic, finally to deliver me safely on the other side of the street. He looked at me with comic disapproval for a moment, and then his olive-tanned face broke out into a huge grin and he began to laugh, and suddenly we were both walking towards the Bazaar, laughing our heads off at nothing.

The Great Bazaar, from its outward appearance, was an insignificant cluster of roofs and dingy streets, crowded out of the scenery by the domes and minarets of the Süleyman Mosque. There was no apparent entrance, for most of the arched doorways lie down back-streets. And perhaps the greatest surprise of all was that, despite its enormous size, it was a *covered* or roofed bazaar, for its Turkish name *Kapalıçarşi* means a closed or covered market.

The building was originally Byzantine, probably the royal livery and carriage stables. When Constantinople fell to the Turks in 1453, these stables were enlarged and converted into a typical Eastern bazaar with roofed streets of various trades, so that at one time there was a Coppersmiths' Street, a Jewellers' Row, and so on. Now, although the old signposts survived, many of the alleys seemed to have lost their exclusiveness and most streets had shops of various trades. Nevertheless, a few old street associations were still apparent, for almost all the leathermakers survived in the same general area, as did many of the goldsmiths and fur traders.

Fortunately, the old Byzantine part of the building was preserved, and was where people had bought and sold weapons and antiques ever since the fall of the city. This was still true today, for the Old Bazaar (as the Byzantine stables came to be called) was still the centre of the 'antiques' and weapons trade, while the New Bazaar had its leather and furniture shops, icons and gold stalls, copper and fur shops, tea and coffee houses. Contrary to popular touristic belief, moreover, the Bazaar seemed not to be merely a quaint Eastern tourist attraction; the Turks themselves now buy many of their everyday needs in the Bazaar, for to them it is a sort of Woolworth, Marks and Spencer, H. Samuel and Sotheby's all in one. Even at the peak of the tourist season, local shoppers always outnumber foreigners.

Mehmet Ali ushered me down a narrow street towards an arched doorway of the *kapalıçarşi*. Then, as he led me through the portal, I was plunged into a different world—the roar of traffic and the shouts of street urchins were instantly drowned in a sound barrage of Turkish music, water sellers' cries, the babble of business, and the din of people shouting. Everything blazed with colour and movement, and I wondered if I had not, for a moment, inadvertently stumbled upon Aladdin's Cave. I saw a fountain of cool, cascading water, where men sat washing their feet. To my left a street of glittering jewel shops beckoned temptingly. Someone on my right tried to sell me a pair of Turkish slippers, and might well have succeeded had not Mehmet Ali, who had been watching my fascination with some amusement, suddenly darted off into the crowd. Fearing that I would be left stranded in this incredible jostling crowd of buyers and sellers, I rushed after him, pushing my way through scores of little boys selling everything and anything, trying hard to ignore the old man who offered strange musical instruments, desperately summoning all my willpower to refuse the tiny girl who solemnly pushed out a grubby hand in which she clutched a beautiful bejewelled dagger. At last I caught up with my friend and he grinned at my relief—Mehmet Ali may not have spoken English but he certainly had an effective way of making himself understood!

Finally we reached his shop, and with some pride Mehmet Ali showed me an incredibly beautiful carpet hanging in the window —for he was a carpet merchant, or 'wallah' as my father insists on calling him. I was spellbound by the rug's beauty and intricate working, and was studying its colours when a voice spoke in perfect English:

'That will be 15,000 Turkish lira, say five hundred pounds sterling.' I looked round and found a young man smiling at me.

'How do you do, Mr Craig, and welcome to Mehmet Ali's shop. I am Ara, interpreter and salesman.' He smiled. 'The English never buy such expensive carpets, and the Scots—they never buy anything at all!' And as I protested, he gave me a friendly clap on the back. 'Come on, let's have a glass of tea.'

Several tiny glasses of tea were brought from a nearby coffee shop, and we all went inside for a seat. Then, as Ara was interpreting Mehmet Ali's welcome to his shop, a couple of tourists were seen hovering around the door—in a flash Ara had brought them inside, had unrolled a selection of beautiful hand-made prayer rugs, and was chattering away with the couple in Swedish. Finally, after some bickering and pleading, the visitors went away empty handed, and Ara shrugged his shoulders.

'How can people pay for the work and skill and patience of a whole winter?' he asked. 'I'm surprised at these Swedes though, for they are usually understanding.'

'How did you know they were Swedes?' I asked.

Ara smiled ruefully. 'Business depends on it. If I don't speak to them in their own language *first time* then someone else will, and they won't come to my shop. Then I lose my job.' And he ran his finger playfully across his throat.

'And you speak Swedish?'

'Yes, because the Swedes are good customers. Not like the British who only look but never buy, or even the Americans who buy, but always argue. And as for the *French*! In their raincoats!' He rolled his eyes in mock horror—so presumably the French were not easy customers either.

'So you speak French too?'

'Well you see, I am an Armenian,' said Ara. 'My grandparents left Turkey at the time of the 1915 massacres and I grew up in France. But now that the Turkish government no longer persecutes the Armenians, I have returned to my real country. So I speak both French and Armenian.'

'And excellent English,' I added.

'And German, Italian, Spanish, and Russian,' said Ara, '. . . and now I want to learn Japanese!'

I was staggered. But Ara was right—it was his job, and in the cut-throat business of the Bazaar he had always to be one up on his carpet-selling rivals.

Shortly afterwards a waiter materialised from nowhere.

'Do you want to eat?' inquired Ara.

'Is there a restaurant in the Bazaar?' I asked.

'Oh yes, several, not to mention a post office, barber shops, banks, and a couple of mosques. Most shopkeepers eat and do business at the same time, so this fellow takes our orders every day.'

Mehmet Ali ordered and I was told to wait and see what would come. Soon the waiter reappeared with a tray and Mehmet Ali looked curiously under the various aluminium lids which were assembled in front of him. He lifted one and pointed to some bread.

'*Ekmek*,' he said.

'*Ekmek*,' I repeated, and he beamed. I had spoken my first word in Turkish, and with that we happily sat down to our meal. This consisted of a plate of *shish kebap*, still on its skewer, decorated with parsley, green peppers and tomatoes. This was eaten simultaneously with an accompanying plate of rice or *pilav* (my second word in Turkish), and the whole lot was washed down with a glass of *ayran* or watered yogurt. Finally, lunch was rounded off with large slices of juicy water melon. My first meal was delicious, but as Ara told me later, they were kind to me that day.

Meanwhile, people kept coming into the shop to meet the new foreigner. Some arrived evidently looking for a quick sale, and were angrily turned away by Mehmet Ali, but I did make a number of friends that afternoon, in particular the owner of the alabaster shop next door. He was called Yilmaz, was my own age, and wanted desperately to improve his English, which had not yet got past 'Very nice alabaster! Very cheap! You want to buy, mister?' So we made friends and promised that we would teach each other Turkish and English.

Yilmaz had some very beautiful wares for sale, and when I held some onyx vases up to an electric light, the greens, yellows and douce greys were really gorgeous, sparkling and glancing in veins which no marble could match. My great regret is that I never bought any alabaster.

Later in the afternoon we took a walk round the Bazaar. I soon realised how fortunate I was to have such an expert guide, for the place was a maze of intricate passages and streets. But I felt safe following in the wake of my new friend, and he seemed pleased at this opportunity to improve his English. He soon proved to be of still greater value, for before long I was entranced by the Bazaar's magic, and Yilmaz had difficulty in stopping me from buying all sorts of things. What became clear, however, was that the Bazaar was also one vast chum club: when I wanted to buy a dagger, Yilmaz revealed to me that his 'brother' sold cheaper knives. His uncle, I later learned, sold cheaper hookah pipes, and his cousin, of course, sold particularly cheap painted plates. By the end of our tour, I figured that Yilmaz must have been related to about half the Bazaar.

In fact, the prices in the Bazaar were not as great as people suspect. It soon became clear, from watching Ara selling carpets, that prices varied according to the impression created by the visitor. I once saw a carpet sold to a friendly honeymoon couple for only a few pence profit, while on another occasion an aggressive American paid twice the cost price for his prayer rug. Yilmaz, who had a great love for children, sometimes sold his beautiful alabaster to them at only cost price, and when asked why, he would say simply, 'Allah taught me to.'

As evening fell, the Bazaar began to grow quiet. There was a last rush of buying around six o'clock, then people seemed to go home, leaving the Bazaar's businessmen with a relaxing hour in which to have a last glass of tea and a quiet conversation. Then one by one the lights went out, leaving only a few merchants still counting their day's earnings. At around seven-thirty, the city watchmen arrived and at last it was time to leave. The door of the Great Bazaar swung shut behind us and was locked, and as suddenly as I had left the world outside, seemingly ages ago, so I rejoined its terrible traffic, its urchins, and its noise.

Ara left us, and Mehmet Ali and I had a meal in a busy street restaurant. Somewhere above us I could hear a *muezzin* singing from the balcony of his minaret, his voice lost in hopeless competition with the traffic below him. The evening was warm and we sat together for some time, Mehmet Ali content to let me absorb the sights and sounds of his city. Veiled women stopped and stared, and some approached begging for alms. Innumerable children seemed to run around the streets, unattended by parents; I saw one little boy happily playing with a hoop and stick and others playing marbles among the passing feet. Then eventually even the traffic began to thin, and I saw a camel being led through the twilight towards some back-street yard.

Reluctantly, we left for the hotel. The oily proprietor was still there, sitting with a group of men in the street outside, participating in the general Turkish custom of enjoying the evening warmth. Then Mehmet Ali looked at me for a moment with more of his mock seriousness.

'*Iyi geceler*,' he said gravely.

'*Iyi geceler*,' I replied with equal gravity. And off he went, laughing at my attempts to say goodnight. And I went to bed and dreamt of cockroaches.

2 *Living in Istanbul*

Istanbul is one of those cities which you either love or hate. You either accept its squalor and poverty along with the beauty of its mosques and fountains, or else you are repelled by the sight of old men bent double under huge loads, of legless beggars propelling themselves by roller-skates fastened to their limbless stumps, of the drop-outs of European society hanging around the area of Sultan Ahmet, still searching for *hashish* despite the vigilance of the police. Somehow, within this city of contrasts, there is no room for feeling neutral.

And yet, even had I disliked Istanbul, there was an irresistible urge to visit its past, to pry into the world of the Thousand and One Nights. Walking around the legendary harem of Topkapi Palace, now a vast museum of incredible wealth, I found myself surrounded, not only by overweight Americans with cine cameras, and sun-blistered English ladies with floppy hats and printed dresses, but also by those same drop-outs who haunted the Sultan Ahmet quarter nearby. Strangely enough, *everybody* wanted to imagine themselves back among the rose-scented gardens of the harem, watching veiled ladies from some discreet observatory, sharing with them the fear of the guards with their fierce moustaches and curved scimitars, scenting the fragrance of sherbet water or coffee brought on trays by slave girls. And amazingly this atmosphere of the past still pervaded even the brashness of Coca-Cola vendors and postcard sellers now usurping the quarters of the harem's beauties.

The city was also said to boast over six hundred mosques. Many survived virtually unchanged from the days of the Sultans, hidden among grubby back streets or slowly crumbling apart among the washing lines and dusty tracks of the city's shanty quarters—if only visitors could unearth those tiny corners of Ottoman life! But of Istanbul's mosques, only a handful seemed ever to be visited by tourists, for whom tall minarets and vast domes were clearly more photogenic than dilapidated cupolas lost in dingy forgotten areas of the city.

To the tourists, the most important mosque was the Sultan Ahmet, sometimes called the Blue Mosque because of its predominantly blue interior tiling and paintwork. Although Istanbul's faithful still regularly attended this, the St Paul's Cathedral of Turkey, they seemed to be lost among the hordes of visitors who daily trooped in to erect tripods, pace out distances, or shout at children who had strayed off. Somehow, because it was not a church, tourists seemed to forget that the mosque was nevertheless a house of God, and I found myself distracted by the trivia of thoughtless people invading the sanctity and quiet of a house of worship.

Yilmaz took a day off work, and together we visited the Blue Mosque, still his favourite in spite of its tourists and postcard stalls.

'Do you see the six minarets?' he asked me. 'They are very unusual in the world of Islam.' I asked why, and discovered that according to old Islamic law, mosques were supposed to have had no more than four minarets, because the greatest of all mosques, at the tomb of Mohammed in Mecca, had five.

In 1609, however, the architect Sedefkar Mehmet Ağa submitted to the Sultan Ahmet I his plan for a new mosque. Sedefkar had been instructed to design a mosque with golden minarets—in Turkish *altin* minarets—but he mis-heard *altin* for *alti*—the Turkish for *six*. The Sultan fell so much in love with the design that he decided to defy Mecca, and built the mosque with six minarets—so in Mecca they added two more minarets to the mosque by the tomb of Mohammed, and it has now seven minarets! And so Sultan Ahmet built the only mosque in the world with six minarets.

We entered by the main portal, past the front courtyard with its fountain and beggars, past the queues of foreign women waiting for cloaks with which to cover their bared shoulders, past the stall selling miniature Korans, postcards and slides. Removing our shoes, we pushed aside the heavy curtain at the door, and found ourselves suddenly under the immense roof of the mosque The entire structure was supported by four colossal pillars, giving the impression of a vast floor space and inspiring still greater wonder at the acres of carpeting which covered it. Here, to my mind, was the ultimate combination of Turkish workmanship—wonderful carpeting, Iznik tiling, precious ivory, mother-of-pearl inlay, exquisite marquetry, Marmora marble—a mosque fit for a sultan. Beside the pulpit or *mihrab* was the royal box, where the sultans could enter on horseback, and beside this were the two most enormous candles I had ever seen; indeed the whole tone of the building was one of vastness and grandeur, sensitively lit by two hundred and sixty tiny windows built all round the domes and half-domes floating above. Little wonder, I thought, that official pilgrimages to Mecca used to begin here.

But the Sultan Ahmet, though by far the most popular mosque for tours and excursions, was by no means the city's only regal mosque. The Süleyman Mosque, built for Sultan Süleyman the Magnificent, was possibly the most supreme monument in the entire city, the result of the genius of Sinan, Ottoman Turkey's most famous architect. Yilmaz and I used to sit in its courtyard, admiring the magnificence of rising tiers of cupolas and domes, listening to the *muezzin* calling in the evening glow, watching the pigeons strutting proudly along the steps of this awe-inspiring mosque. Inside, we found four tremendous granite columns—one from Baalbek, one from Alexandria, two from Byzantine Constantinople. We discovered the tombs of Sultan Süleyman I and his wife, in lovely sixteenth- and seventeenth-century tiles. We met the caretaker, who demonstrated the mosque's unusual accoustics by clapping his hands and smiling as the clap became suddenly amplified into a roar of cannon. We discovered a tiny corner of old Ottoman Stamboul by gazing over the city from the terrace behind the mosque. Who, I wondered, could remain unaffected by this mosque?

From the Süleyman Mosque, standing on the rising hill of old Istanbul, we could see the minarets and domes of many other mosques, each with names ringing of history. Below us, by the bustling Galata Bridge spanning the Golden Horn, stood the Yeni Mosque, a seventeenth-century building where we went to feed pigeons and watched men washing their feet by the fountains under the mosque's walls. Yilmaz laughed at my amazement. 'We Turks may look dirty and unshaven, but at least we keep our feet clean!' he explained.

Further up the Golden Horn rose the Eyüp Mosque, once the grave of Mohammed's standard bearer, who died during an Arab seige of Constantinople in 669. The caretaker told us that the sultans used to come here upon their accession to the throne to strap on their swords. Nearby stood the Fatih Mosque, one of the oldest and most interesting of Istanbul's places of worship, for it was once not only a house of God, but also a school and seat of learning: at one time Fatih was a vast complex of buildings, incorporating not only the mosque itself, but also various *medresses*, or seminaries, tombs, baths, kitchens, and even a caravanserai.

Then we rejoined the tourists again. Like the Sultan Ahmet mosque, the Church of Aya Sofya was especially noteworthy for its vast floor space, created by massive columns supporting the central dome and numerous half-domes. We hovered round a guide standing under the huge central dome, enjoying the attention he was receiving from a group of Germans, but his recitation of dates and names and dimensions seemed to strip the building of its vigour, and we left to do our own exploring. We discovered the great gallery with its frescoes of St John the Baptist, Christ, and the Virgin Mary—the pick of several newly-resurrected and preserved paintings recently found beneath layers of Ottoman plaster. And what fantastic stonework—brought by Justinian from Rome, Ephesus, Heliopolis, Athens, Baalbek and a dozen other pagan temples. We craned our necks looking up at the dome, twice destroyed by earthquakes, and twice laboriously rebuilt by the Byzantines. We recalled the pillage of this wonderful church by the greedy soldiers of the Fourth Crusade, and contrasted their awful behaviour with the later decorations provided by Mehmet the Conqueror and his Ottoman successors: the preservation of the mosaics by Sultan Mehmet II, the enormous ablution urns given by Murat III, Ahmet III's central chandelier, and the two gigantic candlesticks donated by Süleyman the Magnificent. But somehow the guide droning on beneath the dome seemed to depress us, and we left, somewhat disappointed by his inability to make the museum come alive, retaining only our own private visions of Mehmet the Conqueror, captor of Constantinople, riding proudly into this great church on his white charger.

From this fabulous example of Byzantine skill it was only a short distance to the Topkapi Palace, a collection of seraglios wherein sultans trembled at the sound of the assassin's footsteps and beauties learned the art of pleasure, awaiting the day when they, out of a harem of over three thousand women, would be summoned to the royal bedchamber. We paused to admire Sultan Ahmet III's fountain, stranded outside the palace ramparts, and then obediently joined the tourists filing through the outer gate of this, one of the world's most amazing museums.

Between the palace's outer and middle walls were the Church of Saint Irene—older than Saint Sofya, and in many ways also more serene and agreeable—and the palace's artillery collection, the cannon lying green with weathering under a copse of trees in the gardens. I discovered several of the more interesting weapons hidden away in a disused courtyard behind St Irene's church, and wondered why these had not also been put on show; it seemed wrong that cannon should have been stored in a churchyard.

To call Topkapi a 'palace' would be wrong, for the buildings were actually a series of small seraglios all collected within the safety of the three strong defensive walls. The site, on a promontory of land dividing the Golden Horn from the Bosphorus, was occupied successively by pagan tribes, the Romans, the Byzantines, and the Ottomans, and assorted ruins were on show around the palace's various courtyards and in the neighbouring Archaeological Museum.

The present museum combined some of the world's most important treasure collections within a number of rooms reconstructed or maintained in old Ottoman style: several kitchens and private quarters preserved exactly the sumptuous surroundings which sultans must once have enjoyed while meeting foreign ambassadors. Much of the palace seemed to echo with the fear which must have surrounded those who lived within its grim walls, and the perpetual dread of murder and intrigue was reflected by such names as Executioner's Fountain, Dead Men's Gate, and the Cage. Now, however, all was peaceful, and the various gardens and pools lay shaded by plane trees. Were it not for the tourists, the place might even have been beautiful, despite Topkapi's riot of architectural styles.

Topkapi was fortunate in one major prospect, for unlike St Sofya, it had never been sacked or ravaged other than by small fires. Incalculable wealth was lost, for example, during the looting of Constantinople by the Crusaders in 1204, and then by the Turks in 1453, but Topkapi, a later building, survived, preserving the best of all that was Ottoman, reflecting the varying whims, for example, of many sultans—from Selim III's love for music to Murat III's taste in tiled walls, from the same Murat's fashionable tulip-motifed robes to Murat IV's gold embossed armour.

Here also were preserved some of the world's most fabulous art collections: porcelain of the greatest Sung and Ming, Sèvres and Dresden: precious jewels, countless as grains of sand upon a beach: colossal emeralds almost as big as golf balls: pearls and rubies plastered on to thrones and innumerable weapons as if mere scraps of glass: the fabulous 86 carat Spoon Diamond, ranked high among the world's greatest stones—so much wealth that I cannot even recall how I felt on looking at it. Here too was one of Europe's most magnificent armouries, with gold-engraved muskets and diamond-encrusted scimitars apparently so plentiful that only a fraction of the palace's collection could be put on show at any one time. Stored in vaults and in the Library was the greatest known collection of Ottoman miniature paintings, with over ten thousand exquisite examples now rescued from the dingy recesses of half-forgotten reading-rooms. On display in the palace stables stood an absorbing collection of Ottoman coaches, among them a carriage built for some sultan's favourite lady, complete with latticed windows so that no one could see her face. Elsewhere was a collection of costumes worn by some of Turkey's greatest sultans: the gowns once used by Süleyman the Magnificent: the robe worn by Mehmet the Conqueror when he died in 1481: the kaftan, stained with blood, in which Osman II is alleged to have been murdered in 1622.

Perhaps the most important part of the Topkapi museum was its restoration of the Harem. In the nineteenth century, when the royal residence was superseded by the new Dolmabahçe Palace, the Topkapi building became the exclusive quarters of the Harem, save only for a few black eunuchs retained to guard the women. Here, then, lay the focus of ambition for every beauty living under Ottoman rule, here the death of many a girl's unfulfilled, ungratified hopes. Here in the Harem were the secret tunnels through which sultans crept when visiting their favourites. High above the women's baths was a secret window from which sultans could observe their beauties at play: high above the Bosporus was the window from which so many girls were thrown to their deaths, tied up in sacks and cast into the channel's stormy currents. Here in the Harem was the very centre of the Ottoman Empire during its crumbling, decaying decline, where sultans, drugged with power and drunk with pleasure, watched an empire slither through their groping fingers. To revisit the scene of so much intrigue was a strange experience . . .

Somewhat incongruously, this same scene of wretchedness and pleasure was also once a centre of religion, and in a quiet palace kiosk, beside a gently tinkling fountain, lay the Prophet Mohammed's cloak, preserved in a golden casket and worshipped by those Faithful who came to pass by. Here also were the carefully preserved swords of the Prophet and his four leading followers, Ömer, Osman, Ali and Abubakr, together with the Prophet's longbow. And meanwhile tourists gloated over gleaming diamonds, eyed wicked-looking daggers, smirked on being shown the Harem quarters. How paradoxical!

The museum's site at least afforded an excellent view of the Bosphorus, with Anatolia jutting through the haze beyond. Wearily (for Topkapi was a big place), Yilmaz and I sat down below a tree and watched the ferries zig-zagging urgently across the crowded waterway towards that mystical continent of Asia. How I longed to see for myself the homeland of the Turks, the plateau from whence flowed those carpets which I had seen sold in the Bazaar, those jewels in Topkapi's treasuries.

That evening, while having a meal at the Bazaar, Yilmaz asked if I wanted to visit the night school where he had learned his English. I grinned, reflecting that his teacher had failed somewhat if, after more than a year of study, his pupil had not yet progressed beyond 'very cheap alabaster . . .' However, we soon set off.

Yilmaz's night school was buried away in a dingy Istanbul back-street with no lighting, seemingly miles from anywhere; and I began to admire my friend for coming so far out of his way just to learn English. However, on arrival, I found an enthusiastic class of about twenty youths and girls, all in the same position as Yilmaz, with day-time jobs and only their evenings free. And yet, here they were twice a week, desperately keen to learn English and prepared to pay their teacher's high fees. I was assured that this was by no means unusual; similar schools existed all over Istanbul, said Yilmaz, all trying to cope with the sudden demand by Turkey's youth for lessons in a variety of foreign languages. I felt almost embarrassed to admit that in Britain such enthusiasm was seldom found, but no one seemed surprised.

'You see,' said Yilmaz, 'the Turkish republic is a new country. In the days of the Ottoman sultans, there were few schools and no lessons in languages, except Arabic, which people learned in order to study the Koran. But now Turkey has to win a place in the modern world—not with guns and bombs, but with the enthusiasm of her teachers and her youth. If we Turks want to make our country a great one, we must improve her trade, her industry, her tourism. And so we have to study English and French and German.'

I remembered Ara, bargaining in Swedish, learning Japanese, and I wondered if Britons had not perhaps become too complacent.

We arrived just as the class was ending, and I was soon surrounded by students, all eager to test their English on the visitor. One fellow introduced himself as Volkan, a university student taking English lessons in order to be a tourist guide in the summer. Eventually, when we had shaken off the rest, Volkan, Yilmaz and I were able to leave for a walk around this unfamiliar part of the city.

Volkan took us to what he called a 'wedding salon'—a suite of

View of Ortahisar protected by its 'castle'

An early photograph of myself with the Algan family

rooms designed especially for wedding receptions, Turkish style. As I later learned, weddings in Turkey vary in custom from place to place, and we had in any case missed the actual ceremony: by now, the relatives of both families had been introduced to each other, initial reservations had been drowned in wine and *raki*—a rather potent aniseed drink—and a gay, rip-roaring party was in progress.

As we pushed the entrance curtain aside, we were met by a tremendous roar—Volkan had arrived! He laughed, and introducing his friends to the crowd, found us a table from where we could watch the proceedings.

'You see,' he explained, passing me a glass of rose sherbet water, 'a wedding is a very special occasion in Turkey, and so we have a cabaret . . . oriental dancers, folk-singers, jesters and magicians, and a little dancing.' Volkan was suddenly interrupted by a strumming of Turkish instruments and a clamour of tambourines, and in a flurry of skirts and veils there appeared a girl, warmly greeted by the crowd, writhing and twisting in time to bongo drums and vigorous strings.

'You didn't say anything of belly-dancing,' I laughed.

'Oh no, this is not belly-dancing,' said Yilmaz. 'This is known as Oriental dancing. It looks very similar, but you will notice that she never uses her tummy muscles at all . . . it's all a matter of supple body movements, artistic arms and legs.' He broke off to applaud a sinuous backward movement which the dancer had just completed, and continued, 'You will see that there is much more movement around the floor, and that she is also playing tiny brass castanets between her fingers . . . to a Turk these are important differences . . .' Suddenly the girl's head appeared below Yilmaz's chin, wavering like a cobra poised to strike, her arms performing intricate patterns before his eyes. Laughing, Yilmaz pulled out his wallet and stuck a banknote on her hovering, perspiring brow. It remained there for some time while the dancer rewarded his generosity with some more supple movements and wiggles, and then it vanished suddenly into her costume, as she went off to tantalise someone else. Eventually, having accumulated some considerable wealth in the recesses of her bosom, the dancer disappeared behind a curtain, leaving an enthusiastic audience clapping wildly.

There followed a jester of sorts, apparently hilariously amusing though I could not understand why. His main claim to fame, I felt, was that he performed the most incredible dances while still maintaining his comical fooling. When later I met him, I discovered that, behind his mask, he was about sixty years old! Was he perhaps the last exponent of an ancient tradition, dying out in an era of modernity . . . the sad, forlorn fate of an old jester, reluctant to retire because he knew that when he went, a way of life would perhaps go with him?

I was thinking about this when Yilmaz pointed to a small stage. 'Now we have Western music,' he announced proudly, as a 'pop' group of sorts appeared and began fiddling around with amplifiers and guitars. Unfortunately, their music was, by Western standards, roughly three or four years out of date, but some people seemed to enjoy it, and a few danced in ungainly fashion on a small floor.

It slowly began to dawn on me that the crowd was unfamiliar with this type of music. Only the young seemed entertained, or indeed tried to dance, while their parents sat back, paying mere lip-service to the innovations of the West. I glanced at Yilmaz—his generation would find considerable parental opposition in trying to Westernise Turkey, I thought, if this was all that the West could offer.

So it was with great feeling and emotion that I tried to prevent Volkan from suggesting to the assembled crowd that I should join the group performing on the stage. I had only once mentioned my guitar, but in a fit of amiable drunkenness, Volkan recalled this and gleefully announced it to the entire crowd: suddenly everyone was pressing me to play. Desperately I pleaded I had no guitar—and was promptly provided with one by a member of the group. In agony I insisted that I knew no songs, but they said that all I need do was play. Protesting wildly, I was pushed on to the stage and introduced to the various youths in the band. And then Volkan, in a moment of raki-lubricated triumph, formally announced the guest appearance of a famous British 'pop' star, and left me to my own devices, stranded on the stage under the curious gaze of the elderly, applauded and screamed at by what now seemed to be vast hordes of Istanbul's youth. Limply I asked the lead guitarist what he wanted to play, and to my relief he suggested several tunes which I knew, so for the next ten minutes I was left to stumble through the band's mistakes, before an audience which was growing steadily more and more receptive, while I reflected on the reception we would have enjoyed had all this been in Britain. I imagine we would have been booed off the stage.

After several hours of torture, it seemed, we finally ground to a ragged halt, to a bewilderingly tumultuous reception from the crowd—I could only feel that they were mad! This, however, was only the beginning of Volkan's doings, for no sooner had I stepped off the stage than he announced that I would now sing—an announcement which was greeted with such approval that I decided it would be useless to argue, despite my poor voice. So wearily I trudged back to the stage, and found the guitar thrust back into my hands. Another summit meeting was called in which we discussed what songs both the band and myself would know, and eventually we settled for a few well-worn melodies. With this, the entire pantomime began all over again, the band making its usual mistakes, the singer desperately trying to remember the words of long-forgotten songs, inventing them on the spur of the moment when memory failed.

Finally, in the very early morning we escaped the revelry and celebrations of the 'wedding salon'. If I had learned but one thing, it was that I would never again advertise my guitar! The initial problem, however, was how to get back to the hotel, for virtually the whole of Turkey shuts down at about eleven at night, leaving only a few weddings and tourist night-clubs still disturbing the peace. Fortunately, a *dolmuş* appeared, so we all piled in, and with much hooting and screeching of brakes as the driver made the most of the city's deserted streets, we set off for the Lale Oteli.

The Turkish dolmuş deserves a special mention, for it is one of those institutions without which I would have been lost and totally stranded on many an occasion. The dolmuş is generally a large vintage American car, painted with a distinctive yellow or chequered band around the body-work, and noted for its breed of incredibly skilled but maniacal drivers. Like all Turks, dolmuş drivers are fatalists—having carefully painted *maşaallah* (if God wills it) above the windscreen, they then get on with business and leave the rest to destiny.

Dolmuşes cruise around most Turkish towns, picking people up and setting them down again wherever they want. You simply yell where you want to go, to any passing dolmuş, and if your destination is in the same general area as that of the passengers already inside, you quickly hop in before the police book the driver for stopping in an unauthorised spot. Normally, dolmuşes are only supposed to carry five people, but they often carry more. The useful thing about dolmuşes is that there are so many of them; indeed Istanbul city council has long been wanting to ban them from the streets in order to improve the traffic problem, but it is said that they are reluctant to bring the issue to a public vote because of the sheer numbers of dolmuş drivers.

Eventually we arrived at my hotel, whereupon Volkan announced that tomorrow he wanted to introduce me to friends of his living on the Anatolian side of the Bosphorus—here at last was my chance to visit Asia! Suddenly another night of cockroaches, yet another breakfast of runny jam and olives, seemed but a small price to pay for an escorted trip into Anatolia.

How long it now seems since Volkan and I first went into Asia, and how disappointed I was to find that nothing was different. Save for a barren backcloth of dry, dusty hills, there was little to distinguish Asiatic Istanbul from the mass of apartment blocks and spindly minarets clustered on the Bosphorus's European shore —how disappointing.

We travelled by boneshaker bus to Bostanci, a quiet fishing village on the shores of the Sea of Marmara opposite the Princes Islands, lying quietly off-shore. There in Bostanci, I was introduced to Volkan's innumerable friends, played innumerable tunes on someone's guitar, drank glasses of tea, and eventually was introduced to the Algans, a family living nearby.

Turkish hospitality has for centuries been generous if not

excessive, but on this occasion it surely outdid itself, for the Algans promptly laid on a fabulous feast in honour of their visitors. Daughters were packed off to the kitchen where they prepared a host of traditional dishes; father Algan dutifully passed round the raki; coffee was brought on little trays and was carefully consumed so as to leave the dregs in the bottom of the cup; and then with much ceremony the menfolk sat down to be entertained. One daughter performed Oriental dances, and Volkan was delighted that I could now tell the difference from belly-dancing. Another daughter presented us with sweetmeats and pastries, and a third refilled the raki glasses. I felt almost like a sultan.

What an evening, and what a party! I danced Turkish fashion, but had my revenge by teaching the Turks the Highland Fling. Once more I played the guitar, but was rewarded with a lesson on the sas—Turkey's traditional stringed instrument, similar to the bazouki and the balalaika. I was plied with endless stuffed peppers and vineleaves, pastries and aubergines, sardines and yogurt, and I in turn invaded the women's kitchen sanctuary to show them how to cook scrambled eggs. Eventually I was asked to stay for the remainder of the night, and I protested in vain. Then, almost with the inevitability of fate, one night became three, three became seven, and soon the offer of a week was lengthened to a month. Eventually, with excitement stifling the initial embarrassment of accepting the Algans' offer, I bid a fond farewell to the Lale Oteli, its oily proprietor and loathsome cockroaches. I caught a stuffy little ferry for Asia and moved in with all my baggage as guest of the Algans.

From the start, I was accepted as a new addition to the family. Mrs Algan became Selma *anne* or 'mother'; I called Mr Algan Şefik *baba*; Ayla, Ayfer and Merih became my sisters, Nezih my brother, and granny Algan, whose hand I reverently kissed and pressed to my forehead, asked to be called *anne-anne*, or grandmother. And with this formal introduction began a long friendship with the Algans.

Bostanci, though a relatively peaceful fishing village, lay nevertheless on the fringes of Asiatic Istanbul, and as such housed a predominantly suburban population. Şefik *baba* himself was an electrical engineer, handling large contracts among the new factories and plants now being built around Istanbul. The Algans had actually been city dwellers for some time, though they had also owned estates in Egypt and Greece. Those days were gone and the family now lived in suburban Bostanci, but how surprisingly conservative were their attitudes, and how little changed their way of life, in spite of having lived for several generations in the city.

Algan living had many paradoxes—inevitably perhaps for a traditional family beset on all sides by the values and materialism of the West. I was, for example, never left alone *in public* with any of thc Algan daughters, for Turkish girls have long been barred from contact with single men before marriage. But within the house, I could talk and eat with those same daughters and no one would mind. It was a curious schizophrenic situation—the three Algan daughters generally dressed in the newest European fashions when going for a walk, and yet refused to be seen alone with me! I attended a local wedding where there were many similarities between the Turkish and British marriage ceremonies—was this another step towards Westernisation? It was not. I was told by the groom that, although the registry-office service might seem to have become Westernised, he still intended to be the traditional head of the house. Indeed, he would *shoot his wife on the spot* if he ever came home to find her with another man, even if only *talking* to him!

I was also never allowed to make my bed or to tidy my room—for these were jobs performed only by women, and no man would dream of doing them. Similarly, though I was an honorary member of the family, I could not make myself a sandwich or a glass of tea without causing horror among the women (who would fly to do these things for me), and very strong disapproval among the men (who found themselves faced for the first time with someone who actually did not mind the shame of performing domestic chores among the womenfolk).

And as I lived on among the Algans, more examples of submerged conservatism rose to the surface, like flotsam bobbing up to the surface of the sea—dislodged by some disturbance in the waters below. Eventually, however, I decided reluctantly to leave

Bostanci: I had come to Turkey to live among the villagers of Ortahisar, and comfortable though my existence in Bostanci may have been, it was not the purpose of my trip. Nevertheless, I had learned some Turkish, and I had gained an insight into the things which offended conservative Turks—points which I knew would stand me in good stead in Anatolia. Eventually I caught an overnight bus and settled back for the long journey to Ortahisar—and the strange 'Valley of the Fairy Chimneys'.

3 *The Valley of the Fairy Chimneys*

I travelled all night from Istanbul, in a bus packed with people curious to meet the infidel sitting among the men-folk on the back seat. We passed through Ankara in the dead of morning, a few lights twinkling in the grey dawn. As the light became clearer I was roused from sleep by the sight of a mighty volcano rearing above the road in front of us—Hasan Daği, permanently snow-capped, and majestic over Anatolia's dreary plains. The bus swung east and climbed into hills, then soon we descended once more into the little township of Nevşehir, overlooked by a simple Seljuk fortress—one of the ugliest and least interesting towns in Turkey. It was about six o'clock, and people were already up and going about their business. A market was in full swing, and in the morning light piles of vegetables were being unloaded from lorries ready to be sold—huge cabbages, many over two feet in diameter, carrots over eighteen inches long, baskets of apples and quince, grapes and apricots, cucumbers and tomatoes. I was amazed that the apparently dry and dusty land around the town could support such a variety of produce.

Nevşehir was the official terminus, but for those people prepared to pay a few more pence the bus would continue as far as Ürgüp, fifteen miles further on, calling at Ortahisar on the way. I paid the extra money and began gathering my baggage together as the bus set off again. A weak sun struggled through the morning grey as the scenery became bleaker and still more parched. And then quite suddenly, with unexpected drama, we passed round a bend and I had my first glimpse of the 'Valley of the Fairy Chimneys'.

It was a sight never to be forgotten, a landscape of melancholy and weirdness, quiet in the pale pink of morning. Wave upon wave of rock, sculpted by nature into incredibly surrealistic fantasies, rolled off into the horizon; clusters of tall, pointed rocks huddled together in miniature forests; hidden valleys meandered here and there in abstract, meaningless courses, suddenly losing themselves in still more cross-currents of finely polished waves of stone. By the road a cluster of cones spired into the sun, their needle tips capped with crazily balanced boulders abandoned in some freak of erosion, each one threatening at any moment to fall off, but none ever doing so in the months that I knew them. Here, one forgotten ravine glowed a warm honey colour, another stark white; beyond, a clutch of cones reared red into the sky, while by the road the rock seemed pink. What more fiendish creations could nature devise? What stark, yet strangely appealing simplicity in that riot of colour and geography.

Seconds later the white-capped cone of Mount Erciyas appeared on the horizon, almost silhouetted by the rising sun behind. Someone on the bus explained that Erciyas, spewing dust and lava in the Tertiary Age, had caused the soft tufa rock now so strangely moulded by nature into 'the Valley of the Fairy Chimneys'.

'Why "the Valley of the Fairy Chimneys"?' I asked. My fellow traveller smiled.

'Some call this place the very jaws of Hell, others the meeting place of the Gods. We Turks prefer to call the tall cones of rock the *peribacasi*, the "Fairy Chimneys".' But he would not enlarge upon this, and I never discovered where fairies fitted into the history of this savage, stark corner of Cappadocia.

I was still looking back at the fairies' rocks and cones when the bus swung abruptly off the road and soon stopped in Ortahisar. A minaret was moaning, tea-glasses were clinking, donkeys brayed, and a few curious heads looked out of someone's tea-house to inspect the new arrival. My baggage was stacked up on the street, and with a roar the bus went on its way again, leaving me alone in this strange village with my guitar and luggage. Somewhat bewildered, I gathered up a couple of cases and made for the inn, where I was met by the proprietor whose first suggestion was that I have a glass of tea. Gratefully, I received one and as I drank, I signed the register.

'Aah, *doktoroğlu*!' smiled the proprietor knowingly, and his son ran off to tell the village that the *doktor*'s son had arrived. Before long I was surrounded by a group of grinning, silent villagers, simply watching me drinking my tea. One finally asked, was my father the *doktor bey*? I nodded, and they smiled happily. 'He was very good to us,' said one fellow. 'You will have many friends here.' But then hospitality overcame their curiosity, and I was allowed to go to bed for a much needed rest, while in the tea houses and barber shops, Ortahisar discussed the arrival of the *doktor*'s son.

I was roused by a knocking at my door, and a young man came in with some tea.

'Hello,' he smiled. 'I think you will be wanting this after your journey.'

I grinned, delighted to find someone who could speak English, for a month with the Algan family had taught me but simple Turkish. And with that began my friendship with Tahir.

Outside, life was in full swing. A dolmuş was preparing to leave, and its driver was shouting for more passengers. There were sounds of glasses chinking and dominoes smacking, and below my window someone was arguing over the price of apples.

'Come,' said Tahir. 'I will show you my village.'

The most striking feature of the village's geography was an enormous fang of rock which towered two hundred and more feet above the main street, and which was pitted with strange holes and tunnels.

'That is Ortahisar's "castle",' explained Tahir, and I was surprised how easily I could follow his Turkish. 'People used to shelter here from their enemies, especially the Arabs, who used to raid Cappadocia during the years of the Byzantine era. Indeed, *Ortahisar* means the "Middle Castle"; you can see the first one on the outskirts there, and the third is at Uçhisar, another village near "the Valley of the Fairy Chimneys". Between them, the three rock castles protected the local population during times of danger.'

We climbed to the top for a view of the village. The castle had already become something of a tourist attraction, being a landmark which could be seen for miles around, but I was surprised to find a secure stairway winding up through the fang's deserted tunnels and crevasses. Half-way up we met Kemal, a little hunchback who had the honour of being called the Keeper of the Castle

—for a hunchback he had remarkable agility, and made sure that Tahir and I reached the top safely, all the time chattering on about his past life, when he had been a film star in Istanbul.

The view from the top was fabulous. Every corner of Ortahisar, every secluded courtyard normally hidden from the streets by high walls, was now spread out before us. Apricots lay drying in the sun on flat roofs, and here and there veiled women were hanging up spotlessly white washing. Two deep gorges cut through the village, both virtually dry of water, but poplars grew in their shade, golden leaves flashing in the sun. Someone was leading a string of donkeys through a winding cobbled street and a group of brightly dressed children followed, toy-like in the patchwork of a little toy village. Beyond the children lay the village wine vats, cut deep into the same tufa rock which I had seen so spectacularly eroded by nature in 'the Valley of the Fairy Chimneys'. And adjacent to the vats was a cluster of newly-built houses, strange under their pointed roofs—one sign of the progressive measures slowly being introduced by Yaşar bey, Ortahisar's municipal mayor, I was told.

Tahir pointed to a house on the outskirts of the village, a little bigger than some, with scarlet flowers trailing from a balcony into the courtyard below.

'It's my house,' he announced proudly; and he indicated his mother, veiled in the burning sun, spreading apricots out to dry on the roof. 'You must meet my family, and eat with me tonight.' And a meal of welcome was duly promised for the following night.

Beyond the village, shimmering under the fiery sun, lay the cones and needles of the Fairy Chimneys, and I decided to go back that same day to visit them. Tahir produced a pair of donkeys (I had never before ridden one, but mine was a docile, contented creature), and we set off along the dusty track towards the Fairy Chimneys.

The asphalt road from Nevşehir to Ürgüp crossed our path, its petrol station looking a little out of place in the somewhat lunar surroundings of cones and craters. We passed a motel, then being built by Yaşar bey in an effort to increase local tourism, and as we jogged down into the maze of valleys and needles ahead, Tahir explained the history of the locality.

It is a fascinating battle-scarred, multi-racial one. Stone Age men, Hittites, Phrygians, Cimmerians and Scythians all came as settlers, and all died violently. The Persians came, but were ultimately defeated by Alexander the Great; and when Alexander died on his way home from India, the province passed through yet another troubled period of warfare while various neighbouring tribes battled between themselves for its possession. Eventually, Cappadocia was forcibly incorporated into the Roman Empire, but even when this became part of mighty Byzantium, Cappadocia knew no peace. Arabs, Persians, Egyptians and Mongols all attacked, carrying off young slaves and what little wealth could be found in this, the poorest and most devastated province in Asia Minor. Finally, the Seljuk Turks arrived, but it was only with the coming of the later Ottoman Turks that there was peace, for even during the time of the Seljuks, Cappadocia became the battleground of the rival Danişmend Turks and the Seljuks of Rum.

The only people to survive those centuries of plunder and bloodshed were the Christians, who lived in Cappadocia from the first century until their final expulsion in 1923–4—victims of the Treaty of Lausanne and the exchange of Greek and Turkish populations which followed.

Christianity was first introduced into the area by emissaries sent by the Disciples Paul and Peter—although Paul is more popularly associated with the Cappadocians, it was Peter who actually wrote to them (I Peter 1:1). Following trends already seen in Syria and Jerusalem, the new faith became first established among the slaves and artisans of Kayseri, then the pagan Roman city of Caesarea Mazaca, but soon Caesarea's nobility found an intellectual interest in the new religion and the city quickly established itself as one of the most important centres of Christianity in Asia Minor—eventually it came to be the sixth ranked bishopric in the entire East.

Unfortunately the Romans clamped down. Major persecutions occurred during the reigns of Nero and Diocletian especially, but local governors also oppressed Christianity to such an extent in

Cappadocia that many people fled to the bleak Melendiz Hills in Western Cappadocia. During this search for peace and safety from persecution, Cappadocian Christians eventually discovered the rocks of the Fairy Chimneys, among whose tiny valleys and strange cones they could successfully lose themselves and continue to worship in security. Gradually a troglodyte population of hermits and refugees appeared, living not only in the many caves found all over Western Cappadocia, but more especially among the spires of the Fairy Chimneys. How close to the Creator those Christians must have felt, scratching an existence from the baked dust in this tiny savage corner of Anatolia.

Then, probably in the fifth century, there appeared the earliest Cappadocian rock monasteries—strange underground hand-carved churches built in groups, where the inhabitants lived by rules based on new and revolutionary principles of communal life—rules governed by obedience to the Superior, humility, poverty, and chastity. These rules, now the basis of many monastic orders, were actually invented by a Cappadocian—the famous Saint Basil, from whom Benedict drew when founding his Order in the West some time later. Although Basil's first monastery was actually established in the province of Pontus, it is likely that his ideas, of monks living together in groups governed by a regular daily routine and headed by an abbot, spread to his native Cappadocia very quickly—perhaps even during Basil's own lifetime.

The very first monasteries to appear in Cappadocia were probably established among the Fairy Chimneys, created by the peasants who lived there into what eventually became the amazing complex of rock churches known as Göreme, a collection of chapels and monasteries, dwelling houses and refectories all constructed entirely underground in a series of caves and tunnels.

It was in this community that the Cappadocian monks reached their highest standard of achievement, not only in an exercise of social co-operation, nor simply as guardians of a sanctuary for persecuted Christians, but also in art—for in Göreme there appeared some of the world's strangest murals, and most original architectural plans.

You have to visualise scores of tiny cells, carved from solid rock with only primitive scraping tools, by monks living from day to day under the threat of Arab attacks. By the seventh century, the Byzantine Empire could no longer protect such provincial peoples as the Cappadocians, and with the passing of every decade they came to be more and more forgotten and abandoned. Constantinople ultimately fell in 1453, about *four hundred years* after the capitulation of Cappadocia's cities to the armies of the Seljuk Turks. But in spite of the long occupation of the province by Moslem troops, the monks of Göreme carried on with their duties, offering shelter to refugees, partaking in daily communion with the Creator of the strange surroundings now offering them secrecy, and continuing to enlarge the community's collection of churches and burial chapels.

In spite of Mongol and Arab attacks, Göreme's remarkable monks were responsible for the creation of more than twenty major churches, three monasteries, several large refectories, and even a complex system of cook-houses, bakeries, a hospital and a prison. Quite an achievement! Nowadays, however, the churches have become the main focus of attention.

Created between the fifth and fourteenth centuries, the rock churches of Göreme are now widely regarded as being among the greatest known monuments of devotion to Christianity extant in the world today. The labour and time which must have gone into their creation is incalculable, the quality of faith infinite. Furthermore, Göreme's peasant monks not only produced remarkable rock churches, but in time broke with traditions to create churches of original design, incorporating on occasions such unique features as the triple apse, the double narthex, and the double nave. Moreover, every plan devised by Göreme's architects could be applied to any free-standing church—not bad for rustic peasants! Unfortunately, Göreme's stone masons were less skilled, and sometimes sound architectural plans were marred by poor craftsmanship; domes did not always sit squarely on their supports; arches were not always symmetrical, penditives not consistently shaped. But to criticise such achievement would be unjust, for it would be to ignore the tremendous devotion which every monk, skilled or inexpert, must have felt in his heart when working in Göreme.

The monks were also ingenious artists. Indeed their sensitive mixture of pre-Christian local folklore with later religious paintings left them as artist-monks rated highly among the most original and interesting of Byzantine painters. It seems that Göreme's monks also experimented occasionally with new styles and techniques being adopted elsewhere, one example being in the use of Hellenistic influences. Syrian and Armenian styles were also adopted occasionally, and sometimes with great success, but basically the monks remained in the rut of their own traditional style, unaffected by trends going on in art centres elsewhere. So it was within the narrow confines of their own style that the monks painted, unaware of their contribution to Byzantine art, uninterested in painting commercially, but merely carrying on with their own form of praise to God, decorating their churches in sincerity and uncomplicated piety.

Eventually, Göreme died, partly from lack of communications with beleaguered Constantinople, partly because of thc tolerant attitude which the Turks adopted towards their Christian subjects. Christians were given ethnic and political recognition within the Ottoman Empire by the *millet* system, persecutions died out (except when the Turks lost any of their numerous wars with Russia), and as a result, the Christians of Göreme were at last free to live in normal villages, generally unmolested and no longer needing the uncomfortable caves and rock cells which had for centuries protected and sheltered them. At least the churches would survive, to show historians how Göreme had moved through different styles of architecture and several art controversies before finally dying. One day, tourists would stand baffled among the rock chapels, wondering how people could possibly have created them, or why some chapels were painted with drab ochre while others were so colourful. One day archaeologists would marvel at the monks' skills. Or perhaps the monks prayed instead that no one would ever come to disturb their simple monuments to God. And so Göreme was abandoned, and its churches' entrances were concealed so that no one might destroy the evidence of so much devotion and piety.

Our donkeys began to trot as we descended into the valleys of Göreme. To our left, perched above a miniature canyon, was the Fikretan Kilise, the first rock church I had ever seen, its ornamental façade indicating that it was probably among the last to have been excavated from the tufa. And then suddenly Göreme itself was in sight, and to my intense disappointment, my first glimpse was of a Coca-Cola stand and a car-park—the West had struck again.

'This is what we call progress,' shrugged Tahir. 'Last year there was nothing here but the curator's house; now you have to pay. Last year there was peace and stillness; now you have to queue behind the bus parties. Last year Ortahisar's people were poor; now they are better off.'

We paid and went through a gate into the monastery's precincts. A pitted tooth of rock, once the living quarters of monks, towered above us, and I reflected on the paradoxical situation of having to *pay*, plus extra for my camera, for entry into what was once a haven of charity and the shunning of wealth. Nearby, the Chapel of St Theodore offered frescoes from the early Iconographic era, primitively dabbed on to rough-hewn rock, with occasional early plaster surfaces now damaged by damp. Several graves, now cruelly exposed to passing feet, suggested the church might have been perhaps a funeral chapel at one time.

Tahir indicated the gloomy fresco of a mounted rider.

'St George,' he laughed, pointing to a wriggling dragon. 'Some people say he visited this cave—he was a Cappadocian, you know, and probably lived quite near here. But I don't personally believe that he was anything more than a particularly humane man, whose reputation happened to spread beyond his friends.'

In fact the local legend of St George seemed to have become confused with a number of other 'horseback saints', for we discovered in Göreme alone, frescoes of St Theodore and St Prokopion, also busily spearing angry dragons; while nearby, I was assured, lay another chapel where we might find St Demetrius also mounted and fighting the good fight.

Various other surrounding chapels, their presence betrayed only

Rocks near Göreme

Monastery near the entrance to Göreme

The Dark Church, the dome decorated by a *Christus*

by tiny doors and modern signposts, gave evidence of Göreme's stormy history. The tiny chapel to St Barbara reflected perhaps the community's finest Iconoclastic art, its rough architectural shape and red ochre sketches contrasting vividly with the beauty and grace of its neighbour the Apple Church, an eleventh-century exhibition of bright painting and spacious architecture.

Tahir pointed to a scrawled name carved into a column in the Apple Church.

'Göreme's first tourist,' he laughed. 'Historians say his autograph dates from the sixteenth century.' The sad figure of Christ looked down on us from a Crucifixion scene on the opposite wall, and I wondered how many visitors He had seen since that first adventurer scribbled his name on the pillar.

The Apple Church's great asset was its brightness, compared with many of the surrounding chapels. St Theodore's chapel was perhaps understandably gloomy because of its aura of death and burials, but that of St Barbara, probably once a place of baptism, seemed unaccountably dim inside. The Apple Church, however, was bright and airy, though lit by one solitary window—too many windows would have betrayed the presence of the churches during times of danger. I looked out of this single rock-cut aperture and found myself perched high above a ravine, with a flight of worn-out steps skidding almost vertically downwards from what must also have been the chapel's original door. It became easy to understand the great security once enjoyed by Göreme's monks. The present door must only recently have been carved, for the sake of tourists—at one time the only access would have been up the steep cliff outside. In fact the community must have resembled Mistra in Greece, with entry only by climbing up rock faces where today no one dared to go.

We continued our tour of the churches. The Apple Church, I was informed, derived its 'tourist name' from an orb held in the hand of Jesus, painted in a tiny dome above the altar, while the Snake Church's name came from a prominent fresco depicting St George spearing his dragon, twisting and frothing around his horse—two amusing misinterpretations! This chapel resembled that of St Theodore, for it seemed to date from the same artistic period and may also have been a funerary chapel, to judge from the number of exposed graves. Its frescoes, however, were original, and included portraits of the great founders of Orthodoxy, Constantine the Great and his wife Helene. There were also pictures of two of the traditional horseback saints, Prokopion and George, and an intriguing fresco of a naked man, said to be St Enoyfrios, an Anchorite of the desert.

Nearby stood a fascinating rock refectory, its stone table now beginning to crumble away, its roof partly fallen in. But somehow there remained an impression of jovial Friar Tuck-like monks, all seated happily round their *higumene* or abbot, busily tucking into joints of meat and swilling good Cappadocian wine (which had actually been pressed for centuries before any monks appeared in the area). We later discovered a second refectory, its stone benches partly restored to preserve, virtually intact, the room's appearance as it must have been during the community's later days. Next door were the soot-encrusted kitchens, their baking ovens, fire places, and storage pits for wines and fats still well preserved. Beside the head of the table in the dining hall were roasting hollows, the grooves along which spits were slotted into place still visible, the basins in which fires once burned now cleared of their ashes as if ready for another day. In front of one barbecue pit was a shallow square cut into the stone floor, where grapes were trampled by monks, and from which the juice flowed through a small hole into a handy pit, also dug into the floor. Doubtless the juice was then ladled into vats, where it fermented into Cappadocia's famous wine.

At the head of the table sat the abbot in a special apse carved in the place of honour. He was evidently in charge of all meat carving, for a stone platter, cut into the table, was before his place. Gravy runnels ran the length of the table and finger-bowls were carved into the stone at suitable intervals. Anything could be carved from stone it seemed, probably because wood was scarce; even the monks' benches had marks to show where each man should sit, though either the stone mason had poor eyesight and judgement, or else some monks were considerably more amply proportioned than others! And yet, on a basic diet of only herbs, bread and water—the example set by St Basil and the famous fourth-century 'Cappadocian Fathers'—it is difficult seriously to imagine any of Göreme's inmates being in any way rotund.

Göreme's greatest triumph, however, lay in the creation of the Dark Church, situated in the community's convent quarter. First, however, we climbed to a tumbledown arcade, probably once a quiet ambulatory for nuns but now a broken shelf perched precariously on a cliff-side, a few carved blind arches being all that remained of this nuns' retreat. From this ledge we could see through a solitary window into the gloomy recesses of Göreme's most magnificent achievement, the Dark Church.

The chapel was superb in plan, style and execution. Entrance was now by a narrow stairway cut into the cliff-side, to the level of the nuns' ledge outside, where there suddenly opened to view the vestibule, itself beautifully decorated in douce-coloured frescoes, with the promise of greater glories awaiting discovery in the deep blackness of the church beyond. This vestibule or narthex was probably used as a teaching room for novices, or as a recess wherein penitents prayed, said Tahir. And then we ventured into the darkness . . .

Tahir had been thoughtful and produced a torch, without which it would have been completely impossible to see anything of the church's murals. He flashed a feeble glimmer round the walls—and suddenly the place was transformed into an art gallery of incredible beauty. On one side the sombre eyes of Jesus glinted down at us from a scene of the Crucifixion. From another wall His Mother, serene and beautiful, rested while Salome washed the infant Child. On a third wall, crowds welcomed Christ and the Apostles into Jerusalem.

Though the paintings seemed remarkably similar to those in the Apple Church and elsewhere—perhaps they were even painted by the same monk, for they dated from the same period of the eleventh century—how different they now looked in the darkness, compared to the brightness of other chapels.

Then Tahir's lamp came to rest on one wall.

'These are the finest paintings in Göreme, maybe in the whole of Cappadocia.' Even Tahir, a Moslem, was moved by the quality and dedication in the work. Two scenes in particular were miraculously preserved from damp and vandalism as if by Fate. One, flickering in the dim electric glow of the torch, was a scene of Christ in the Garden of Gethsemene, accosted by Judas and a host of soldiers. What superb passivity, what emotion, was portrayed by that unknown artist. The other, an exciting scene of the Last Supper, was one of several identical murals to be found in a number of churches, but how strangely different it now seemed. The artist *must* have been inspired by the grandeur of the work around him, for this is, I thought, the finest of all the copies extant today.

The scene showed Jesus saying 'The man who has dipped his hand into the dish with me is the man who will betray me' (Matthew 26:23). Judas seemed to be frozen, with his hand outstretched towards a central bowl leaving the other Apostles clearly suspicious, whispering anxiously among themselves.

How this nameless, undiscovered master could have painted *at all* remains a mystery. He had no ready-made paint, no handy sable brushes, no formal art training, not even a full day in which to work, because as a monk he had other duties to perform including six daily calls to prayer. He did not paint in security, for although the eleventh century was one of reasonable calm in Anatolia, the menace of Arab attacks was never far off—and the Seljuk Turks were very soon to arrive. How *did* he manage to paint such anguish, such fear, calm, happiness, the entire range of human emotions? His skill will, I suppose, remain forever a mystery and wonder, and the two simple frescoes on which Tahir's light now rested will remain among the world's least appreciated monuments of human skill and devotion.

Later chapels seemed pale in comparison to this, Göreme's best showpiece, but many still retained their own characters—little facets of the personalities of their long-forgotten creators. In the Church of the Sandals, for example, we found clearly marked footprints scooped out in the floor—supposedly a copy of those of Jesus in the Church of the Holy Assumption in Jerusalem, from which the Church of the Sandals derived its name. In the Buckle

Church, we discovered a tiny room below the main chapel, where wedding meditations and occasional honeymoon nights were spent by lovers now long dead.

The Buckle Church itself, divided into the so-called Old and New sections, also illustrated some of the influences once popular at Göreme; in one part were the remains of Syro-Palestinian styles, for example, while in another were the more Orthodox lines of Constantinople, with scenes usually depicting the main events in the life of Jesus—popular with almost every artist whose work had survived vandalism, damp and erosion.

I pointed to a large hole in the floor of the church, in front of the altar, at which Tahir suddenly seemed sad.

'The churches of Göreme were discovered by Father Jerphanion, a French priest, in expeditions made during the 1910's and 20's,' he said. 'But they were often filled with rubble, and the job of clearing the caves was not undertaken until the 1950's; until then people could only see the ceilings and the upper parts of some walls, and then only by clambering over stones and fallen masonry with powerful lamps. In the 1950's, however, the government excavated the best chapels and gradually Göreme took the shape it used to have before it was abandoned in the fourteenth century. The Buckle Church was cleared in 1955, and, following the discovery of precious relics buried near the altars of other chapels, people were very excited at the prospect of further hidden treasure in this church, especially because it was about the biggest chapel so far discovered. But the whole lot was stolen before the museum authorities could get here to do their own digging. . . . They say it was a passing tourist who apparently spent the night in the chapel, ostensibly studying the newly-revealed wall frescoes, before catching up on his itinerary. The next morning he was gone, leaving this large hole in the church's floor. . . ' Tahir shrugged, 'It's very difficult for us to understand Europeans sometimes.'

We walked out of the church's gloom into the bright sun, searing hot and mirrored off a thousand snow-white needles. The more we wandered around, the more chapels we discovered, until at last I began to feel that Göreme's population must have lived like rabbits in a warren! Life must have been very hard, for nearby a peasant woman was clearing dirt from an irrigation channel built by Göreme's Christians, and further off, a young boy was clambering up the steep side of a cliff towards a tiny bricked-up window—presumably that of some inaccessible chapel.

'No, he is going to collect guana,' explained Tahir. 'It seems that the monks of this region built special cells for the local pigeons, so that they would have dung to use as fertiliser. These little windows, many of them painted with colours believed to attract birds, are the entrances to the "pigeon houses" as we call them, and occasionally, when there is enough guana, small boys from local villages collect the droppings and spread them on the fields, just as they have been spread for centuries.'

Life in Göreme certainly had been difficult, if people had had to collect fertiliser from such inaccessible places, I thought. But in fact, it could have been worse—there was at least an education system, run by monks, which taught boys and girls the essentials of learning, and which also provided lessons in various useful trades, by craftsmen paid by the monks. And the community also looked after orphans, in the ways prescribed by St Basil, founder of Orthodox monasticism. Indeed the monks followed the unwritten rule of St Basil, their great founder and source of inspiration, in many ways—as indeed was fitting, for had not Basil and his fellow 'Cappadocian Fathers' once saved Orthodoxy from the heretics of Arianism?

Tahir pointed to a lonely outcrop of rock, high above the rest of the community and set slightly apart.

'Göreme was a community in every sense,' he said, 'for that was once the prison . . . crime existed even in a religious settlement, it seems.' We climbed up to the cave which had once been the jail, and discovered two chambers, with rough beds carved and hacked out of the rock walls—I supposed that a partitioning door once separated males from females. Scattered ashes indicated that this lonely cave was now the shelter of some shepherd, but he was not in, so we could not ask him how it felt to be living in prison.

Although the main community once lived in fairly closed

surroundings, there were also a number of outlying chapels of unusual interest, many of which were only now being unearthed because of their more scattered locations. The best of these was 'discovered' by Tahir's father, Murat, so we duly set off to find the 'Hidden Church'. The chapel would have been virtually impossible to find had I not been with Tahir, for it nestled under the overhang of a steep cliff. A flight of newly-cut steps made entry from the top of the cliff a little easier, but even these were well camouflaged and blended all too easily into rocky surroundings.

Tahir laughed at my poor head for heights.

'Come on!' he cried. 'The monks had to do this without the benefit of such nice broad steps.'

We scrambled down and entered Murat's church. Having kept my eyes open at Göreme, I could tell immediately that this was a chapel of interesting artistic influences—a portrait of St John in the Desert, for example, included in its scenery needles and cones resembling those of Göreme itself. Some frescoes, including a scene of the Presentation, were Hellenistic in style, while Tahir assured me that there were also Mesopotamian influences in the general style of the church. Most impressed by this intellectual knowledge, I asked him how he knew, and puffing with pride he explained that his father's church had become the sole subject of a book written by two professors from Istanbul University,* wherein all had been revealed and explained. He added that the church was considered to be ninth to twelfth century in construction, but that the paintings were of the twelfth to thirteenth century—indeed they were therefore of major interest because Cappadocia had by then already been occupied by the Turks for well over a hundred years, and yet the Christians were still painting and still surviving. The Hidden Church, he explained, was one of the few known examples of such late painting, and was therefore Very Important! I laughed with him at his mock pride.

Nearby, we discovered the desolate and broken remains of the Ninazan Church, a dumpy cone of rock now sadly exposed to wind and rain, its once-impressive frescoes now scratched and

* Ipsiroğlu, MS., and Eyuboğlu, S.: *Saklı Kilise*, Istanbul, 1958.

faded—the fate of so many unknown or undiscovered chapels now beyond repair. Though I could see that the Turkish government had done much work in preserving what survived at Göreme and elsewhere, how many churches had already been eroded away, taking with their dust and rubble untold masterpieces of art, I wondered.

Tired and weary after a hard day's exploration, we returned to our donkeys. The sun was beginning to set, and the needles and cones of the Valley of the Fairy Chimneys were slowly turning a golden honey colour. Evening falls rapidly in Turkey, and as we plodded back to the car-park, we watched an endless spectrum of colour sparkling and dancing among the cones. Soon the honey colour had blended into a fiery red, reminiscent of a fierce alpine glow. And as soon as the red became deep crimson it slowly began to dwindle into a douce pink, then mauve, and then purple, leaving but occasional tips of tufa bathed in orange. Then, quite lazily and with a silent haunting beauty, the sun's orb sank into the open jaws of the Fairy Chimneys, and a pale purple night fell.

Donkeys plodded past, their shadowy riders nodding in friendship as they overtook us. Further off, voices hummed around the little restaurant—the West's latest innovation to break the sanctity of Göreme. Our donkeys were feeding happily near the car-park, so we went to meet Ahmet the restaurant-keeper, and Ali the owner of Göreme's little trinket shop.

We found them gathered round Ali's kiosk, arguing with a couple of Americans. It appeared that one, a typical Texan, suitably attired with shorts, sun-specs, cigar and movie camera, was determined to buy something *genuine*—it had to be *genoowine*. Ali smiled with content, and in a moment produced a staggering selection of odds and ends—bits and pieces of long-rusted firearms, small copper 'relics' of the Christian era, an assortment of ceramic water pitchers, and a few woollen moneybags. But the Americans weren't interested, and the fellow's wife turned to go—so Ali produced grade two of his wares—a wolf-skin said to have been acquired by the last local pasha, a pair of half-rusted stirrups, supposedly from the horse of an unfortunate nineteenth-century Kurdish raider, golden discs from the ancient head-dress of a village maiden, and a tiny Roman oil-lamp, looking remarkably new and unused, I thought. The wife faltered, glanced at the golden discs, but then moved off once more.

'Wait, sir!' cried Ali desperately. 'I will show you my very greatest treasures . . . the last of my most precious possessions . . . those nearest my heart.' The Americans paused, whereupon, with a display of the greatest possible reverence, Ali unwrapped from the depths of cotton-wool and tissue paper, half a dozen Roman tear-glasses and a solitary Hittite cylinder-seal, beautifully wrought from some delightfully-streaked stone. The wife pounced, caught her prey, and left Ali with a fistful of fresh green dollars. With great glee the two visitors *salaamed* a dozen times, and, barely concealing their triumph, waved merrily until their car disappeared into the darkness of the night. There was a silence. Then Ali looked at Ahmet, who glanced at Tahir, and suddenly everyone was laughing and laughing, the tears rolling down their cheeks as Ali put away the remainder of his precious relics. I never found out if the tear-glasses were real or not—the cylinder-seal was a fake, bought by Ali from its maker for a few pence, but sold for a fortune.

'It is only justice,' explained Ali. 'People come every year to steal from Turkey . . . to buy Turkish treasures, but never to give back to Turkey. Does it matter if they go with a few replicas? What does it matter, so long as our friends are content with what they buy?' He shrugged. 'In any case, it is the Will of Allah.' I was left to ponder over that most ancient of Islamic explanations.

We tethered our donkeys outside Tahir's house and left his sister to stable them. Tahir's mother was waiting for us at the door, and greeted us with welcoming words of hospitality. Following Turkish manners, I removed my shoes, and then replied by kissing her hand and pressing it to my forehead—a hand gnarled and worn from many years of working in fields—hoeing, gathering and threshing are considered suitable occupations for women. Men prefer to exercise their traditional dominance by sitting in tea-houses gossiping.

As Tahir's mother led us into the guest room, I noted that she did not take off her veil—this only happened after I had visited her house several times, and only then if there were no other strangers around. The guest room consisted of a vaulted ceiling and white-washed walls hung with Turkish carpets. A carpet-covered sofa ran along one wall, but nothing covered the bare floorboards. Our hostess spread a blanket on the floor, however, upon which she placed the traditional basin of glowing charcoal, at which we might warm ourselves. We were offered glasses of tea and duly sat down to drink around the basin. Except for Tahir's mother, no other females entered the room—apparently they congregated in an adjoining chamber, wherein no men were allowed to enter.

Having drunk our tea, Tahir produced a large round wooden tray, and placed this on top of a low stool covered with a heavy quilted blanket. We then sat down crosslegged at this low table with our feet nestling against the charcoal basin, while the heavy quilt retained the heat and served also as a tablecloth-cum-napkin. Tahir's mother entered with a tray of steaming dishes, and we were left to feed by ourselves in traditional Turkish fashion—men segregated from the ladies.

Our meal consisted of a rough potato soup taken with pieces of home-baked half-leavened bread, a dish of beans in which floated a few pieces of mutton and potatoes, and some thick syrup-like grape sauce, which we ate with delicious freshly-baked pastries. Everything was eaten from a central dish, from which Tahir and I helped ourselves with spoons and forks—there were no knives.

'It's rather as life must have been in Göreme, don't you think?' said Tahir. Indeed it was: the inhabitants of Göreme had probably baked the same tough brown bread, had probably grown the same nourishing beans, and had perhaps also relied on grapes to see them through the tail-end of many a meal.

'Of course, the monks kept hens, grew apples and pears, and may even have kept cows and sheep,' added Tahir, 'but we also eat eggs and beef, and of course we have *shish kebap*—so really, life has hardly changed since the days of Göreme.'

I thought of those timeless donkeys which had passed us in the gloom of approaching evening, of the laziness of the tea-house and its endless gossip, of the constant struggle to grow a few meagre apples on some precious withered tree. Perhaps, indeed, the essence of life had changed little since the days of Göreme's monks . . .

When we had finished the last of the grape sauce, I left. It had been a tiring day for me, but Tahir accompanied me to the inn, for it is the custom of Turks to take an evening stroll during the warm summer nights. As we passed the restaurant, we could hear someone's loud, rather tipsy, laughter above the general noise of music and clapping. Perhaps life had been the same for centuries even *before* the coming of the monks, I thought. Was it not the Hittites, after all, who first brewed beer in Cappadocia?

4 Life in Ortahisar

Working among the people of Ortahisar soon became easy because the villagers were kind and friendly, but difficult, because each day soon became almost a monotonous replica of the day before. So this is the description of a typical day.

I was wakened by the muezzin's wailing, amplified by loudspeaker from the minaret along the street. Even at five o'clock, people were up and about their business; someone was cursing a stubborn donkey just below my window, and across the street I could hear old Mustafa's tea glasses clinking and the dominoes already being shuffled for an early morning game. Ortahisar was about to face another day, identical to yesterday, and if Allah willed it, the same as tomorrow. I doubted if life in the village had changed much in centuries.

What a change, I thought, from Istanbul. Here at last was the Turkish way of life for which I had been searching, unspoiled since Ottoman times, each day passing in an unhurried, even leisurely rhythm of doing nothing until forced to. What a contrast to Istanbul's hideous traffic and those little boys determined to sell useless plastic gadgets. Here, in sleepy, lazy Ortahisar nothing seemed rushed; even the menfolk, shuffling into the mosque for early morning worship, took their time.

I had hardly dressed when there was a knocking at my door, and I was greeted by two unshaven characters, caps held in hand, bashfully wishing me good morning.

'*Doktor bey* . . .' they began, and I laughed.

'All right Abdulla, you old rascal! I suppose it's the lumbago this time . . .' Abdulla nodded cautiously.

'And what about you then, Ali . . . toothache again?' He also nodded. So I dug into my medicine case and pulled out some ointment for Abdulla and a few Codeine for Ali's teeth.

'But you'll really have to get them pulled, you know. . . . And next time wait until I've had breakfast before you come scrounging!' And off they went, caps still in hand, praising Allah for the generous *doktor*—and no doubt off to the tea-house for a quick business deal over their ill-gotten gains.

Treating the sick in Ortahisar actually proved much easier than I had at first thought possible. It turned out that on his last trip to the village, my father had written notes for everyone whom he had attended, detailing what was wrong with them. Quite a few people still had these tatty scraps of paper, which made my job of diagnosing illnesses much easier, and also made it simpler to differentiate between those people in real need of my medicines, and those simply trying to scrounge what they could. It was of course also a strange experience, to find all those people with bits of paper written by my father, yet all living so very far from home; every time I saw one of those little notes, I felt a strange communion with my family, and a peculiar confidence would come over me when trying to assess illnesses or discern the skrim-shankers. But with lovable old rascals like Abdulla and Ali, that confidence did sometimes melt a bit, and I would give in to their tragic tales of woe. But it was all part of the early morning routine in the village.

Breakfast usually consisted of a newly-baked loaf bought from the general store, and eaten in the tea-house over several glasses of tea and a game of backgammon with Mustafa the proprietor. The trouble with this was that my diet of tea and bread inevitably led to tummy troubles—sometimes constipation, but sometimes diarrhoea, which was most inconvenient in view of the complete absence of toilet paper in the village.

The trouble with breakfasting in the tea-house was that my games of backgammon were frequently interrupted by people asking either for medicines, or for me to write letters for them. Since quite a number of Ortahisar's villagers were virtually illiterate, it was not long before I found myself popularly elected to the post of village scribe. Ortahisar was a poor village, explained the villagers; its economy depended largely on farming, carpet-making, and whatever tourism it could attract. But the gates of prosperity had now been opened by an arrangement made between the Turkish government and several European nations, for the employment of Turks in light industry, particularly in Italy, Germany Holland and France. Whole families were now moving out of Anatolia and into Holland or Germany, they said, seeking fortunes in engineering, textiles, mining and assembling. One village, I was told, had lost almost all its menfolk to the coalmines of Amiens, while Ortahisar's young men had moved mostly to Holland and Germany, where they earned, by Turkish standards, fabulous incomes. I could see the effects of this for myself—village children were running around in crimplene blouses, mothers were now wearing their traditional baggy pants with ridiculous high-heeled shoes, brothers were sporting winkle-pickers and shortie raincoats over their multi-patched shirts and ragged trousers—all sent from Europe by the village men.

But now, contracts were being completed, work permits were expiring, and the men were beginning to drift back to Ortahisar. And to the horror of wives and mothers, many were returning maimed and injured from inexperience in handling technological machinery. One man had no nose, another no hands; others returned with only one eye, some hobbled on one leg, almost as if coming home from war. And yet, here I was, being asked to write hopeless letters, reapplying for work, asking for an extension to some permit, begging compensation for the loss of someone's hand. . . . Yes, breakfast at the tea-house was often a saddening affair.

Mustafa slapped down his last plastic disc and retired, the triumphant victor of our day's backgammon, and I took a seat by the balcony overlooking the main street. Women were prodding donkeys towards the fields, and in the distance I could tell by its trail of dust that the post van was on its way—perhaps there would be a letter for me. I would soon know by the postman's yelling: people had to go to the little telegraph office to collect mail, for there was no delivery service. Village children dressed in grubby black smocks were heading for the school house, and soon the mini-bus would arrive, bringing its teachers from the local town of Ürgüp.

Below the balcony, a dolmuş was collecting passengers for the trip to Nevşehir, where it was market day, and down the street old Faik was arranging his pathetic collection of antiques under an awning, hoping for a sale should any tourists arrive. Abdulla with the lumbago arrived and shuffled past, guilt written all over his face, and Mustafa brought out his customary bitter coffee and hookah pipe. Eventually more people appeared, and soon almost all the village menfolk were assembled in the tea-house, preparing to pass another day of gossip and backgammon, tea and dominoes. Meanwhile the women plodded off to work, haggard and worn beneath their spotless white veils. The schoolchildren solemnly saluted the fluttering Turkish flag, and disappeared indoors to begin their lessons.

The scene was reminiscent of many a saloon from cowboy films—the honky-tonk piano was now a character playing a badly-tuned sas; poker and roulette tables were domino and backgammon boards; whisky was now tea and coffee. There was the same silence whenever a stranger entered, and while dozens of dark eyes would scrutinise the new arrival from under the brims of battered hats and caps, one or two hands might stray to the hilt of some hidden dagger. Only the frowzy girls were missing—and I thought of the rows of white-veiled figures I had seen working in the fields, a blistering sun overhead, a few mangy donkeys crowding into the shade of some solitary tree. The frowzy girls, I knew, would always be missing.

Then I was greeted by my friend Tahir—the only man in the village who did not wear a cloth cap. His ancestors had all been headmen of Ortahisar in their time, and although his father was now working in Holland, Tahir continued to set his village the example of enlightened living now expected from his family. Sadly, however, nobody seemed to notice his smart suit and polished shoes, groomed hair, or his knowledge of English. And I thought of Yilmaz and Volkan in Istanbul, also trying to enlighten people and to introduce them to the ways of the West, also finding themselves thwarted by a similar barrier of tradition and conservatism.

'My father is an important man in our village,' Tahir once told me. 'He introduced tourism for the first time, and built not only a tourist information office, but also the inn and restaurant. He persuaded the provincial authorities to build the tarred road which runs through the village. He brought relative prosperity to Ortahisar. But now that he has gone to Holland, people have forgotten, and have gone back to their old ways.'

I felt sorry for Tahir, so alone in his way of life, wanting to introduce Ortahisar to the benefits of the West while retaining the best of the East.

Tahir introduced me to Yaşar bey, the present mayor of Ortahisar, a man trying to continue the work begun by Murat, Tahir's father.

'I have built wells and a *hammam* (Turkish bath) in Ortahisar,' he said. 'Every month I motor to Kayseri, the provincial capital, to plead for better roads, and now perhaps we shall have a second tarred road. We are building a new motel to attract tourists, and I also try to keep the inn clean and tidy. I encourage the building of tourist antique shops and coffee-houses—but do the people listen? No, they sit in the tea-houses and in the barber shops, listening to the gossip and the sas as they have done for centuries. It's all they seem to want.'

'Perhaps I can help,' I suggested, not really sure of what I could do, but anxious to maintain Yaşar bey's interest in improving Ortahisar's lot.

'Well, you speak some languages . . . perhaps you could help me to write a brochure about the village. We could distribute leaflets among the local tourism information agencies,' he said.

So Tahir and I wrote a leaflet in five languages, had it printed, and sent bundles to all the local tourist offices. The brochure didn't help Ortahisar's prosperity much, but it was a beginning.

The village inn, built by Tahir's father but now run by the Municipality of Ortahisar, was next on my list of improvements. With Yaşar bey's permission I persuaded its lazy keeper to wash and sweep out the rooms, especially when visitors were expected. I introduced the idea of changing the bed linen between guests, and even managed to have toilet paper installed! Posters of Turkish tourist sites were put on display in the hotel. Rudimentaries like soap and mirrors were added to each room, and a woman was employed to wash linen and towels each week during

The butcher who threatened me with a knife in Avanos

Big Mustafa wearing his astrakhan fez

Avanos, the potter at work

The old 'Byzantine flour mill' at Çavuşin

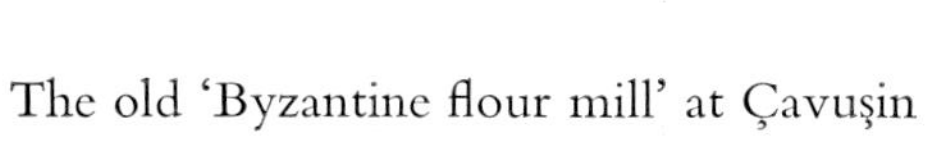

Tourist girl teaching a local how to cook omelets

the tourist season. The innkeeper's sons were enlisted to act as baggage boys and servants, and an arrangement was reached with Mustafa by which he agreed to send tea over to the hotel when required. Inquiries and reservations were answered promptly, if possible in the appropriate language, and the mass of unopened letters which I discovered in the proprietor's desk was carefully sifted and answered where possible. Letters were sent to local tourist offices, urging them to recommend Ortahisar's little inn whenever they could.

For some reason, however, nothing seemed to happen. There was no improvement in custom, no rise in the pathetic number of tourists—and no corresponding improvement in the village's economy. Somewhat mystified, Tahir and I set out to discover the reason, but it was, in fact, not hard to find—the local tourist information offices now resented Ortahisar's sudden modern touristic commercial outlook, and were deliberately diverting potential custom elsewhere. Innkeepers in surrounding villages were now bribing tourist information officers to avoid mention of Ortahisar's little hotel. In fury and frustration, Tahir and I wrote off to the appropriate authorities, who had the culprits removed and the information offices restaffed with more suitable people. With the police now also alerted, more tourists began to appear in the village and a greater degree of prosperity slowly began to spread throughout the whole of Ortahisar, as tea-houses and antique shops did better business. Guides were needed, horses and donkeys were required for hire. Parties were held at the inn and tourists were provided with costumes for the occasion—these were sometimes hung up for sale the next day and were frequently sold for good prices. Carpets, hand-made by Ortahisar's villagers, were hung on the walls of many bedrooms and in the hotel vestibule, and before long I found myself conducting a vigorous business in prayer rugs, between villagers and visitors.

Turkish rugs (*not* really 'carpets') are the result of centuries of knowledge and skill, passed down by village womenfolk ever since the first intrusions of Turkish nomadic tribes on to the Anatolian plateau, in the eleventh century. Nowadays, though some rugs are manufactured in modern factories, many are still woven in remote hamlets like Ortahisar, where villagers follow traditional local patterns and produce distinctive regional types and weaves: even the most inexpert tourist can tell at a glance the coarse weaves and colours of an Isparta carpet from the sheer quality of one from Kayseri or Bursa.

Rugs are generally made during the winter, when most Turkish villagers are snowed up for many weeks, and when there is nothing else for people to do. The early part of winter is spent in preparing colours and dyes, if these cannot be bought. In many villages, rose or tulip petals are crushed for their reds, vegetables are used for their greens, and even urine is sometimes required for yellows and mixing. Then, having manufactured sufficient dye to last a complete carpet (for if it runs out, the chances of making a new batch of *exactly* the same shade are virtually nil), the village women construct their frames, arrange their threads and wool, and set about the laborious task of tying the thousands of tiny knots which constitute a rug. They follow detailed patterns, normally handed down from generations past, and through the winter each household creates a rug, or perhaps an identical pair, in a pattern found nowhere else in Turkey—every peasant women creates something completely unique.

In the spring, carpet merchants from Istanbul travel around villages like Ortahisar, buying batches of carpets and taking them off to be sold in city bazaars to tourists. The price paid to villagers is normally somewhere between £6 and £15 depending on the tightness of the weave, the closeness of the tufts, and the size of the carpet. No wonder Anatolian villagers are poor. I have often wondered how Istanbul's merchants can put such a low price on the laborious work and patience of an entire winter, the infinite skill of generations.

Having been taken to the bazaars of Istanbul and Izmir, the rugs are either sold direct in shops or are put up for auction, to be sold to tourists thereafter at an average price of about £35 for a rug approximately 1¼ metres by 80 centimetres . . . I thought of the gorgeous carpets I had seen sold in Mehmet Ali's shop, and wondered how much had been paid to the villagers who had woven them? But perhaps the most ironical twist of all is that, on one occasion, a British customs officer volunteered to value one such prayer rug, woven in a Turkish village and sold in Istanbul's bazaar for £35. Its value, he declared, was between £400 and £450!

By urging Ortahisar's villagers to sell their carpets in the hotel, not only was the inn decorated in quaint traditional style, but people also got fairer prices for their work, for I made sure, having learned from Ara's example, that visitors paid prices in keeping with their own wealth.

With the coming of more tourists, carpet sales went up, and the news spread to surrounding villages. Soon there was actually a stock-pile of rugs waiting to replace those which were sold. With more tourists arriving, more parties were arranged, and occasionally local village dancers and musicians were brought in to entertain visitors. Sometimes, if the hotel was full up, people stayed in villagers' homes, so bringing a little extra money to needy farmers, and a taste of peasant living and hospitality to their lucky guests. Occasionally, on festive occasions, visitors were invited into village homes to share in celebrations, and I would find myself sitting cross-legged round some table, wine flowing, village food in abundance, translating for some totally bewildered tourist the various phrases of greeting and welcome.

The favourite meeting ground of tourists and villagers was the restaurant, a rather grubby place built downstairs from the inn. As is common in all Turkish restaurants, visitors were invited to inspect the kitchens, where they could choose their food from a variety of steaming pots. There was a surprising selection; soup of the day was often a delicious lentil with a little yogurt added on top; meats usually included *shish kebap*, meat balls grilled over charcoal, lamb chops, liver, and heart; vegetables normally comprised tomatoes (stuffed or simply boiled), aubergines, paprikas, various beans, and peppers; and of course there were always pilavs and salads. Wine, pressed in the village vats, was roughish but tasty, and bread was *always* delicious. Various sweetmeats could be brought from a pastry-shop along the street; nuts for nibbling with raki were provided by the general store, and

Mustafa ran a profitable business ferrying coffees and teas when needed.

The inn's residents generally fed in the restaurant downstairs, where it soon became an established custom to provide music for dancing whenever there was a crowd big enough to make a party worth while. Ali the restaurant owner turned out to be a skilled dancer, and would accompany himself with a rhythmic snapping of wooden spoons while somebody played a sas. And 'Big Mustafa', an extraordinarily colourful character and the local self-appointed wolf, would entertain any young ladies present with his particular brand of Turkish dances—somehow he always managed to contrive many intricate movements with his arm round his partner's waist—but only when his partner was female!

Big Mustafa was Ortahisar's resident showpiece, a man of whom his village was justly proud, but who had acquired his notoriety by breaking every taboo in the book, from drinking where he wanted, to making the most obvious of passes at visiting women, no matter their age, nor even if their husbands were present. To begin with, he was a Turk of unusual height and tremendous dignity, with a fierce moustache and furrowed brow, normally hidden by the brim of a battered old hat—when he was not sporting his astrakhan fez. He was always clothed in virtual rags, but these generally went unnoticed because of a fascinating multi-coloured cummerbund hung with chains and silver trimmings which he wore around an ample midriff. He never told me if he really kept his dagger there, but it was said that he carried both a knife and a revolver, buried in the folds and hangings of this cummerbund.

Mustafa's speciality, second only to seducing ladies, was in acquiring anything and everything that people wanted. I once expressed an interest in antique guns, and in a matter of hours he had called me to his cellar and was unwrapping an extraordinary collection of revolvers and shotguns, crowguns and blunderbusses. On another occasion I was looking for a paraffin lamp, and again he was immediately able to offer me a wide selection of storm lanterns! Later when on the lookout for horse brasses and stirrups on behalf of some tourists, there, true to form, was Mustafa, sidling up to me in the tea-house with an armful of the very brasses which I sought.

Above all, however, I had to admire Mustafa's technique with the ladies. He would introduce himself to any unsuspecting couple simply by pulling a chair into their table, producing a bottle and three glasses, and offering his bewildered hosts a glass each. He could always rely on the fact that visitors never quite knew how to refuse without causing offence, and would therefore accept his drink. Then, having made the innocent victims his drinking buddies, Mustafa would call for music, whereupon sas and bongo drums would promptly strike up, always on cue; and with fierce eyebrows but a charming smile, Mustafa would demand a dance from the young man at his table. Now his victims would not only be out of their depth, they would also be indebted to him for their drink, and his young man would almost always sheepishly rise to imitate Mustafa's dance steps. After a while, with his young victim beginning to grow confident, and now showing off to his wife, Mustafa would call the girl over, would discard her husband, and would craftily alter the dance so as to end up with his great arm round the poor girl's waist—Mustafa enjoying every cheap thrill, his victim totally unsuspecting of all that was going on, the restaurant's door and windows lined with admiring villagers. The whole thing, though innocent enough, was nevertheless highly amusing to spectators lucky enough to be 'in the know', and of course, with every success, Mustafa's reputation grew bigger in this, a village where in the normal course of events there was absolutely no social intercourse between the sexes. So, monotonous though many days may have been, village life did have its funny moments.

5 *Guiding Tourists*

I sat on the balcony of Ortahisar's tea-house chatting to Tahir, who had just defeated me in a close game of backgammon. Below us, the mini-bus was about to leave for Ürgüp, a melon seller was arranging his wares in a pile on the main street, and a solitary car stood outside the inn—two Germans were spending a week in Cappadocia, exploring with Teutonic thoroughness every hidden gully, every innocent village which they could find, returning each evening to the restaurant tired and rather dusty. It would have been wiser, I thought, to have employed a guide.

Autumn had been very hot but as the weeks passed and the threat of winter approached, fewer tourists came to visit Ortahisar, and the inn now looked deserted. In a way this was welcome, for during the busier days of the summer I had been unable to sleep for people wandering around during the night, looking for the loos, or banging on the front door after an evening with Big Mustafa and his wine.

Many people used to arrive apparently expecting some kind of Hilton Hotel, instead of Ortahisar's simple little inn. I had had to reply several times to letters beginning, 'Dear Sir, Please reserve a room with double bed and private shower/bath . . .' and I used to wonder at the number of people who must have been disappointed on arrival to find the village's hotel, so incredibly plain save for my newly installed carpets and posters, lacking any luxury beds or private showers, with the manager probably snoozing disinterestedly under a floppy hat on the hotel verandah.

'But this is Ortahisar,' said Tahir, 'and people must not come here expecting to find Miami. . . . It saddens me to see those visitors, for so few of them are really interested in my village, even in my country. . . . They come only to film and to do as they please. They do not care if they offend our women by photographing them, nor if they sadden our men by paying low prices for everything they buy—to many people Turkey is still an underdeveloped country where the normal rules of courtesy can be ignored, where they can meet the natives but never lose their own "civilised" customs among themselves. It is sad, for we are also civilised, and we too have dignity.' I thought of lecherous Big Mustafa, or Ali laughing over his precious trinket relics . . . were their feelings not basically the same?

In the distance we could see Tahir's mother, married to progressive Murat, but herself timorously veiled, refusing to eat with us, refusing even to remove her veil in my presence.

'My mother,' explained Tahir, 'is like every Turkish village woman—she is shy and conservative, proud and hard-working. She cannot change as quickly as her menfolk do, for she has retained a different love for all that is Turkish and Islamic. . . .'

I remembered that she had still not allowed me to take her photograph, but Tahir explained that this was also because of deeply sown convictions—to a Turkish woman, the belief is that she will lose part of her soul to her image, in photograph or portrait—a reminder of the general Islamic law against the portrayal of any living creature in art or decoration.

'Perhaps it is a hangover from bygone days,' shrugged Tahir, 'but at least my mother is *sincere* in what she believes and does. Unhappily, few Westerners think of this . . . they laugh, or inspect with curiosity our quaint customs, but seldom do they respect them.

'You have seen for yourself how they scorn our little inn, how they film our frightened women and grin as they run off, how they come to buy our antiques and rob us of our history. But have you seen anyone admiring our country, or praising its people, or trying to understand our ways?' I confessed that I had not—I even felt guilty myself.

We looked round as two strangers suddenly entered the teahouse. A deadly silence fell—for one was a girl, and until then I doubt if *any* female had ever entered the male sanctuary of the teahouse. They were British—I knew from my brief training at the Bazaar in Istanbul—so Tahir and I watched with interest to see how they would acquit themselves while under the scrutiny of a dozen pairs of dark, menacing eyes.

They acquitted themselves excellently. In ten minutes both had enjoyed the strongest of Turkish coffee, both had savoured the bitterest of Turkish hookah pipes (offered to them for a joke which backfired because the strangers actually *liked* it), and the fellow had quickly demolished Big Mustafa in a game of backgammon. They were about to leave again, having drunk their coffee, when Tahir suggested that I offer them my services as a guide.

'*What?*' I demanded incredulously, 'I'm not a local . . . there are plenty of villagers here who can guide.'

'No, no,' insisted Tahir. 'You know Göreme as well as any of us now . . . after all, we've been there several times already. And you understand the churches and their paintings better than us, because you are a Christian. And you speak better English too. . . . Go on, ask them!' Tahir grinned, and pushed me towards the departing strangers. And thus began my career as a guide.

My first expedition took place the following day. My first clients were the two strangers who had so unceremoniously invaded the tea-house—and my first pay was a drink in the restaurant that night, chased by a few more provided by a smiling Mustafa, delighted at another opportunity to act the noble villager.

Roger and Margaret introduced themselves as merely 'passing by'—they were actually hitch-hiking to New Zealand on their honeymoon. To begin with I confined our visit to Göreme and its immediate environs . . . this at least provided custom for Ali and his trinkets, for which he was grateful, and for which I eventually won his friendship and a small commission as sales rose.

Having visited the most interesting of Göreme's churches, we continued deeper into the Valley of the Fairy Chimneys and discovered the tiny village of Avcilar, sometimes also called Maçan. The story goes that Maçan derives its name from the early Greek name *Matianni*. It is believed that St Hieronymus, the supposed founder of Göreme, lived in this village, for in his *Acts*, he was the first to mention *Korama*—generally accepted as the old name for Göreme.

Apparently old Hieronymus was chased as a debtor into the maze of cones and needles of rock, where he discovered an inaccessible cave in which he could hide from his pursuers. This, it seems, set the precedent for rock living in the area. An alternative local legend states, however, that the precedent was made by a family who had one of their dead entombed in an enlarged cave buried deep among the cones of the Fairy Chimneys. In any event, we had fun wandering around the rocks, wondering which could have been that early refuge of Hieronymus, or which might have been the first burial cave. But a hoary old villager informed us that wherever it had been, it perhaps no longer existed. Everything, he told us, gets eroded by time, and for all we knew, we may even have walked across the sand and dust that was once the rock cave of Hieronymus.

Was he simply being helpful, I thought . . . or was this old man yet another local resenting the intrusion of unsympathetic foreigners, stumbling over his laboriously ploughed fields, and plucking his carefully tended grapes?

We pressed on to Uçhisar, the most obvious landmark for miles round the Fairy Chimneys, where the village clustered round two enormous fangs of tunnelled rock towering high over the surrounding needles and cones. I recalled Tahir explaining that Ortahisar meant the 'Middle Castle'—here then was the 'Third Castle'. The rock was divided into two towers, the Çavuş Hisar and the Ağa Hisar, which along with the 'castles' at Ortahisar, probably protected the local area's population during times of danger in bygone days. According to locals, their use even extended into the Byzantine era, when attacks from the Arabs in particular made Cappadocia a dangerous area.

We heard rumours of plans for a vast tourist club with all kinds of diverse entertainments and premises to be built in Uçhisar, but when we tried to find out more in the tea-house, the chatter fell into a morose melancholy.

'Of course, we would like to have the money. . . .' said one old man, the apparent spokesman for many of his friends. 'With the money, we could build many good houses and roads, and a hotel in our village . . . but we do not want to lose Uçhisar. If these tourists come . . . if they build their hotels here, we will never again know Uçhisar, and our children will never know our village. They will find only a collection of houses populated by tourists from many parts of the world.' He looked reflectively into a coffee cup, as if trying to read his fortune from the grains of sediment lying there. 'I think we would rather have a poorer village, with no hotel, no good roads for our dolmuş—and no visitors to mock our traditions.' His friends nodded in unanimous agreement, and as we took our leave of the tea-house, one called out:

'Remember this day, please, for if you ever return you may never again see Uçhisar. . . .'

A large hotel complex, run by the Club Mediterranée, has since been built, and the old village of Uçhisar, with its way of life, is fast disappearing. Such is progress.

We walked back to Avcilar, where we hired three donkeys from the same old man who had told us of St Hieronymus. There being no restaurant in Avcilar, we decided to continue to the village of Avanos, where, we were assured, we could buy a meal. So off we set again, into wastes of sand and scrub ahead. We soon moved out of the area of the Fairy Chimneys, and although our track lay along the edge of one long outcrop of needles, we were soon travelling across semi-desert. The sun shone mercilessly, as in all good cowboy films, and indeed, as we jogged along, we began to feel rather like actors in some western. Somewhere in the jungle of rock to our right there must be a 'baddie', waiting to pounce on us with masked face and loaded six-gun.

It wasn't a 'baddie' but an old woman who unexpectedly appeared, riding her donkey out of a narrow crevasse among the needles, singing to herself as she trotted along. We actually heard the singing first, and just as we were beginning to substitute our visions of cowboys for a scene from *Lawrence of Arabia*, this little old lady appeared on her donkey. As she passed us she pulled her veil more tightly about her, and with only one eye visible she continued on her way.

'Are we on the right way for Avanos, old lady?' I called after her, but she never looked back, and we were left to continue by ourselves.

Then quite unexpectedly we came across a mighty river, flowing through the dryness in a dark brown sluggish ribbon of glistening water. This was the Kizilirmak, the Red River, one of Anatolia's great rivers. For centuries this river was the saviour of farming on the barren plateau, was the valley by which many trading routes made their way into Asia Minor, was perhaps the most fought-over frontier on the plateau.

A score of little boys were playing in the shallow waters by the river bank, while beyond lay the roofs and minarets of Avanos. As we crossed by a modern bridge, I wondered how many previous bridges had been built across the river at this point—for Avanos was a village with a long history.

As a bridge point, it may have existed even before the appearance of the Romans in Cappadocia—Herodotus writes of battles being fought between the Persians and the Lydians in the fourth century B.C. specifically for control of the bridges which linked their two empires. Later, Avanos became the centre of Greek Orthodoxy, for the Christians who had once lived in Göreme and similar monasteries eventually became Turkish citizens under Ottoman rule and soon learned to live in tight little communities, rather lost among so many Moslem villages. Avanos had been one such community, its Greek name being probably Vanesa or Vanessos.

I thought of the few remains which now survived to tell the tale of Orthodoxy in Cappadocia—the most important were probably architectural. Cappadocian houses were built of stone, for example—a habit introduced by the Greek Christians—which gave many poor villages an air of definite prosperity. Avanos was one such village—the *shapes* of the houses were now different, but the *idea* of building with stone survived, while in neighbouring provinces the Turks still built with mud-baked bricks, wood, or fired bricks later plastered over. Close to the bridge we even discovered what was probably a former Greek house; its stone had been painted blue and its roof was now crowned with a stork's nest, but the architecture and wooden balcony were perhaps Greek.

We wandered on into the village's market square. Men sat under trees, drinking coffee and tea. A woman jogged by on a donkey with another in tow staggering under a mammoth pile of brushwood and firewood, recalling the scarcity of wood in sun-baked Cappadocia—perhaps that was why the Orthodox Christians had used stone. A crowd of schoolchildren scurried off into the distance, all dressed in grubby black smocks and looking forward to their lunches.

We also looked around for somewhere to eat, and discovered no less than *three* restaurants facing on to the main street—this put Ortahisar's meagre little establishment most definitely into the shade. I chose the least pretentious, mainly because it looked the cheapest, and with great authority I led my two employers into the kitchen at the back, where we were welcomed by the chef and the restaurant-keeper, both of whom were amazed at tourists coming into their place instead of the flashier *lokantas* next door. Having chosen from foods on show, we sat down to a meal of lentil soup with yogurt, grilled meat balls with rice and stuffed tomatoes, melon, and a bottle of local wine to wash the whole meal down—thrown in for nothing by the restaurant's owner.

Then we set out to explore Avanos. Fortunately it was market day, and although most wares had already been sold, the bazaar still offered a few melons, a selection of woollens, some butcher meat, and a some lemons. I decided to photograph the meat, which was encased in some sort of pepper preservative, so I asked the owner of the meat-stall if he would pose for a picture alongside his wares.

He smiled and lifted his butcher's knife.

'Take that photograph and I will kill you . . . with this knife!'

I blinked, shrugged hopefully, and asked him again, more politely, to which he began to wave his weapon threateningly. Fortunately some of his friends appeared and asked what was annoying the butcher, and laughing at his protestations they eventually persuaded him to pose with them while I took the photo. But the butcher never let go of the knife, and even as I took the picture he waved it alarmingly. Somewhat relieved, we made a hurried exit for the village potter's cellar.

We found the potter sitting by his wheel in a vaulted cellar, surrounded by scores of his wares—water pitchers of various sizes, bowls for storing grape juice, smaller jugs for olive oil. Smiling as we entered, he bade us watch him while he turned a pot. To us laymen, he appeared to begin with a shapeless lump of clay, but in seconds even this had been transformed into the obvious beginnings of a water pitcher. Gradually, under the careful hands of a master craftsman, the shape improved; the body appeared, and did not collapse, the slender neck was formed and did not fall lop-sided. And as the shape evolved, the hands kept moving, adding clay here, scraping it off there, sometimes pressing more firmly, with the dexterity and certainty born only from an ageless knowledge and timeless craft. Then finally, with a careless flourish, there appeared a deftly-painted band of colour, and the spell was broken. . . . The potter seemed satisfied, and held his creation up for inspection before placing it carefully among a hundred more identical pitchers. The entire operation had taken less than four or five minutes.

We discovered the kiln outside. This consisted of a vast oven, fired with sawdust provided by the local joinery, in which the pots were stacked neatly in tiers by the potter's assistant. A huge pall of black smoke hung over the kiln, indicating, I was told, that the fire had only just been set alight, and that it would therefore be some time before the pitchers inside would be ready. Meanwhile a couple of characters busily shovelled sawdust into the kiln's fiery recesses.

We wandered back along the main street, trailing our donkeys behind. Then just as we were about to recross the bridge over the sullen Kizilirmak, a young man approached.

'Would you like to see Turkish rugs being made?' he asked.

Roger and Margaret said yes, so we followed our new acquaintance up a few back streets and stopped finally outside a courtyard door. Our guide led us through the area beyond and on into a gloomy room wherein sat his entire family, the women working at a loom against one wall, the men smoking or playing with a few grubby-faced children in a corner. Everyone looked up as we entered, and the women immediately pulled their fallen veils around their faces. Our guide told his family that he had brought the visitors to see carpets being made, but the entire family looked sullen and unfriendly, and I began to feel uneasy and something of an intruder into this private Turkish world.

'Could we take photographs?' asked Roger in bright innocence. I winced, and watched suspicion deepen in the surrounding faces. And then I had an inspiration . . . remembering the assorted British sweets which I always kept at the bottom of my camera satchel, I produced, with great glee, a few simple rolls of sherbet sweeties. The eyes of the children lit up, and one toddler held out his hand hopefully. Delighted, I enthusiastically pressed some sherbets into the outstretched paw, and glanced quickly at the surrounding men-folk—still ominously sombre and unfriendly beneath their skip caps. But I continued to push sweets into the hands of the children, and tried to ignore the threatening men-folk. The children seemed delighted, and so, pleased at my success, I recklessly went on to offer some to the silent women working by the loom. They all looked towards the men, still sitting morose in a corner, but eventually, with what I thought was reluctance, they timidly declined. But I insisted, and desperately rummaging for some more, found some Dolly Mixtures and also offered them around.

One old lady then graciously accepted, and with that the spell broke and the rest of the women also took some sweets. With women and children munching away happily on sherbet cachous and Dolly Mixtures, the men began to look uneasy, even vaguely envious; clearly they had never had to deal with this kind of experience before. So I offered the men the remainder of my sweets—and with cautious reserve, they eventually accepted. Soon everyone was happy and I was fishing sweets out of my Lucky Bag—wine gums, Edinburgh rock, Berwick Cockles, fruit pastilles—all helped to ease the tension.

Eventually we re-emerged from our unexpected sally into a Turkish home, Roger and Margaret richer by a carpet saddle-bag, and myself with a number of photographs now safely on film. As we went off in the direction of Göreme and Ortahisar, the family came to their courtyard gate to wave a fond farewell, and perhaps to lick their sticky fingers.

We visited one more place of interest while in Avanos—the

marble and onyx works. This tiny workshop lay close to the river, from which it presumably drew the water necessary to cool the lathes used in fashioning the locally-quarried marble, alabaster, and onyx. We found no pressure put on us to buy anything, and indeed the workmen seemed glad we were at least showing interest in their craft.

As the men turned shapeless pieces of stone into recognisable objects, then polished them on more refined lathes, I recalled Yilmaz, working in the Bazaar at Istanbul, explaining to me how the colours could be improved by holding the stone close to an electric light, telling me that he sold his wares at cost price because he loved children, introducing me vaguely to far-off Anatolia from whence came his beautiful bowls and vases, cups and saucers. Here then was Yilmaz's Anatolia, just as Mehmet Ali's Anatolia lay within the walls of the carpet-maker's house.

I left Avanos, happy at having discovered a few more tiny corners of a Turkey which was fast disappearing.

That night a great party was held in the restaurant, laid on by Big Mustafa for Roger and Margaret. People even arrived from neighbouring hamlets for the occasion, which was presided over by Mustafa at his greatest, his most swaggering, his most colourful. He put on a clean shirt for the occasion, and ultimately he even donned his precious astrakhan fez for the evening, though as he feared, it was eventually trampled underfoot in a mêlée of dancing villagers. Musicians appeared dressed in traditional costumes and brought with them instruments long forgotten in Istanbul—strange stringed violins, steel banjos, double-ended drums, and the now familiar sas, the mainstay of Turkish instrumental music.

A tremendous dinner was prepared by Ali, the restaurant cook, while Mustafa arranged a long table at which sat Margaret (naturally next to Mustafa), Roger, Tahir, myself, Mustafa's uncle, and a number of other lecherous but jovial villagers. Soups, pilavs, various meats and vegetables, sweet pastries, and a dozen more dishes came and went, and all were washed down with plenty of Mustafa's wine. And then, as the coffee was passed around, the musicians struck up, and soon everyone was whirling and finger-snapping with an expertise acquired only after a few glasses of Mustafa's booze. Tahir proved himself an excellent dancer, and indeed Roger and Margaret also did well, thus maintaining the respect which they had acquired by their success in the tea-house the day before.

As the music grew louder and Mustafa more devious, the restaurant's windows became steamed up, and the crowd of curious faces which had, until then, been pressed against the panes moved along to the open doorway, from which they could get a better view. Mustafa had by now lost his fez but for the moment he seemed to be unworried, as, with Margaret's undivided attention, he produced from the recesses of his colourful cummerbund all sorts of interesting relics. . . . Somehow I thought I recognised the same tear-glasses which I had once seen in Ali's trinket stall at Göreme!

While Mustafa was thus engaged in selling souvenirs, Tahir caught sight of Kemal, Ortahisar's little hunchback and Keeper of the Castle. With a laugh he pulled Kemal from the doorway where he had been watching the goings-on, and offered him a glass of wine.

'After all, we couldn't allow our famous film star to go without a drink!' cried Tahir.

'Actually, one of my films is showing in Ürgüp,' said Kemal.

There was a mini-bus in Ortahisar which, while during the day served as a dolmuş, at night was commandeered for the use of cinema-goers. The spectacle of this mini-bus setting off was an unforgettable sight, for there was no number that it could not take—I once travelled as its thirty-seventh passenger, sitting on the knee of someone who was already sitting on someone else's knee! Meanwhile the young boy employed to shout out the bus's destination, open doors, etc., would hang on happily to the rear ladder, laughing and making rude signs through the back window while we careered through the night towards Ürgüp and its two seedy flea-pits.

Ürgüp's cinemas, like those throughout most of the interior,

Baking bread, village style

A strange industry in Ortahisar, packing ripened lemons in underground caves

Çavuşin, a view of the village

Winter in Ortahisar

had a code of etiquette which was easy to pick up. Families were segregated from single men and youths, presumably to allow young girls to attend without being in close contact with males—even in Ürgüp, where some girls had abandoned the veil, the undercurrent of conservative public opinion prevented them from taking their emancipation any further.

It was most important, when in a village cinema, to give vent to the full range of human emotions during the course of the film. Hence, when the baddie appeared everyone was supposed to join in with a loud and vociferous chorus of booing and hissing. When the young girl cried (as she invariably did), the entire audience was expected to tut-tut sympathetically, and if anyone failed to do so, neighbours who noticed would often demand the reason—I was once jerked back in my seat by a large and grisly farmer who wanted to know why I was unmoved by the sight of a maiden in distress, since when I have always made a point of tut-tutting and booing as loudly as possible. And of course there was *always* a tremendous cheer when the hero appeared, particularly when it was to do his rescue act—what a laugh, watching elderly gentlemen and ruffian labourers all cheering away and tossing caps in the air!

Kemal played the part of a hunchback in the court of a cruel sultan. He seemed to be the emperor's whipping-boy, for he was always being kicked across the screen by this unsavoury character. (I made a note to ask Kemal what it felt like to be kicked with curly-toed shoes.) By the end of the film Kemal had been killed by the sultan for protecting the young maiden, but his death had, of course, been avenged by the sultan's handsome nephew, who was, naturally, the rightful sultan—the wicked uncle having cunningly usurped the throne.

As the film ended, with the impostor being tossed down a bottomless well, the crackling of nuts reached a crescendo as everyone hurried to finish their handfuls of sunflower seeds and pine nuts. Then, as we all emerged from the cinema, rather surprised because the projector had only broken down twice, a number of people actually approached Kemal to sympathise with him for having had to put up with such a horrid sultan! After having received his due of respect and sympathy, we all followed Kemal back into the mini-bus, and with a roar and a toot of the horn, all thirty-seven of us drove off into the black night back to Ortahisar.

Margaret and Roger left the next day. I felt sorry to see them go, for I had enjoyed the company of fellow Britons. We shared a breakfast together, and I produced from the recesses of my baggage my two most precious possessions—a jar of marmalade and a tin of grapefruit juice—which we shared among us along with some bread and an inevitable glass of tea. Then Roger told me that they intended crossing the Turkish frontier into Persia, from where they hoped to make their way to Afghanistan and Nepal.

Eastern Turkey is a savage area of rough mountains, where even the roads run at heights above six thousand feet, so I suggested that Roger should take some of my porridge (my third most precious possession) with him, for we Scots believe that porridge helps to stave off the cold. Roger, I think, found this rather amusing, but I insisted that he *should* take some porridge oats, and the pair eventually left with a plastic bag of oats safely stored in their rucksacks, just in case they should find themselves stranded in the eastern mountains.

I later received a letter from Katmandu, which said that twice Roger and Margaret had been near to exposure and starvation, and had been saved by my porridge—foul-tasting perhaps, but good for keeping out the cold! So in the tea-house, Tahir and I drank a cup of coffee to celebrate my having become a successful guide. As hotel adviser, interpreter-cum-scribe, *doktoroğlu*, and now guide, the world of Ortahisar seemed to have become my oyster.

6 The Underground Cities

The departure of Roger and Margaret marked the beginning of greater things for me, and from then until the onset of winter I began to haunt the inn and the tea-houses in search of more guide work. Generally, I conducted visitors to those sites which I knew well, so long as they included in their tour at least one valley with which I was still unfamiliar. Thus, I added rapidly to my regional knowledge, and eventually I felt able to include more sites, especially on several ambitious tours undertaken during the following spring. In the meantime I used the tail-end of the tourist season to acquire knowledge of churches and castles situated further afield, and to learn intimately the geography of remoter valleys and villages.

Not long after Roger and Margaret left for the wilds of Eastern Turkey, there appeared in front of the inn a large and well-polished motor car bearing a CD plate. Almost the entire village crowded round to see the arrival of this Important Person—there was talk of him being a minister from the government, possibly here to negotiate for a new school—but the new arrival did not even carry a brief-case, for there stepped out of the car a tall, blond fellow sporting casual slacks and carrying a camera. Sadly the village turned away—there wasn't going to be a dramatic moment after all. There then appeared the gentleman's family, and even those villagers who had lingered behind, hoping there might have been something in the arrival of a CD plate after all, silently shuffled back to the tea-house.

The car's owner nipped smartly up the steps of the hotel and disappeared into the inn's darkened recesses in search of a telephone. I ambled in to find him engaged in a fruitless conversation with the innkeeper, for neither man spoke a language known to the other. Sensing the importance of the telephone call, I offered to translate, and introduced myself to the new arrival. Fortunately, the gentleman spoke perfect English, for he was, in fact,

Mr Toyberg Frandsen, the Danish Ambassador to Turkey.

I cleared up the question of the phone call, and eventually Mr Frandsen was able to speak to Ankara. And as a result, I found myself invited to dinner with the Danish party. We agreed to leave soon for a meal in Ürgüp, both in order to find a restaurant better than that offered by Ortahisar (which unpatriotic behaviour disappointed me), and also to discover something of Ürgüp's history (which pleased me, for I hoped to be the party's guide on a trip to Göreme the following day). And a few envious faces stared at the CD plate as our car sped out of sight in a cloud of dust.

Ürgüp, as I explained to the Danes, was a sad and curiously deserted town, which had clearly seen better times. In fact it was once the bishopric of Hagios Prokopios, but the title eventually disappeared during the tenth century, after which, though the town retained the name Prokopion, it degenerated into an unimportant market centre. And with the arrival of the Turks in the eleventh century the town was also stripped of its last administrative importance by the creation of new ministerial offices at Nevşehir and Kayseri, towns which soon became the capitals of their respective vilayets, leaving Ürgüp stranded in between.

Ürgüp *did* remain important to the Orthodox Christians of Cappadocia, however, and the town retained a distinctively Greek look about its architecture: every house was built of stone, following the Greek example, and even now there still remained some examples of Greek-styled columns and decorative plaster motifs, built by later Turks, but including some with Christian crosses! Balconies and doorways were also strongly reminiscent of Greek architecture.

The Christians actually survived in Ürgüp until 1923, when they were sent to Greece in exchange for those Turks still living in Macedonia: the idea may have been hailed as a great example of international co-operation by the politicians who thought of it, but when translated into action, it meant tremendous upheavals and unhappiness for many simple people, and in Ürgüp's case the scar still did not seem to have healed entirely. The town's Greek quarter had, in 1923, been small in any case, but now it was populated by Macedonian and Albanian Turks, most of whom were still poor, having failed to recover fully from that compulsory ejection from their original lands.

Certainly Ürgüp was left a sadder and more desolate place with the final departure of the Christians. The Greeks, though slowly dwindling in numbers, had nevertheless been important contributors to the local economy. Many eighteenth- and nineteenth-century travellers noted in their journals that the Greeks were invariably Cappadocia's most astute businessmen, for example, putting even the Jews out of business! And when famine struck, as it did several times during the nineteenth century, it was the Christians who invariably took the initiative, roaming far and wide over Turkey in search of work while other races apparently did nothing and starved.

It is said that there were also a number of monasteries in Ürgüp, several of which did not close down until the recent expulsion of the Greeks. Photographs of the time which I later saw, showed *papas* in strictly Orthodox beards and habits, posing by fine steps and impressive courtyards—but even these buildings had now mysteriously disappeared, leaving no trace of their former existence, and making Ürgüp all the poorer for their removal. We could only find one solitary Greek house, standing on the road which wound out of Ürgüp towards the village of Sinassos, but its walls and courtyards were crumbling away, and small boys were playing games among the fallen masonry. This was the only surviving evidence, as far as we could tell, of the old days of local Greek prosperity—an entire culture had disappeared.

Now Ürgüp was living quietly. Its economy was clearly beginning to pick up again with the coming of tourism, and for a few lucky innkeepers profits were already beginning to soar. But for most people life seemed to continue unobtrusively: few seemed to have a share in Ürgüp's new tourist industry, and many still set off each morning on their donkeys to outlying fields, to work among their apple trees and vine groves as they had done for centuries.

Although the Greeks were expelled in 1923, there nevertheless occurred in Ürgüp a curiously paradoxical event.

Tradition has it that several Russian prisoners were brought to Ürgüp during Turkey's wars with Peter the Great, and of these a certain John is said to have been the only one who refused to apostatise to Islam, preferring to die a martyr's death in 1738. This John was later canonised as a saint, it is said, after which several miracles suddenly started being attributed to him. One such incident was the woman whose child had been abducted: St John the Russian apparently appeared in a vision and told the mother both where her son's dead body lay, and also who the killer was. Eventually the saint's powers became so well known that a church was apparently built at Ürgüp, some time during the 1890's, with money raised from selling John's embalmed hand to the Russian monks on Mount Athos.

Tradition does, of course, often distort things, and it is in fact more likely that if St John the Russian existed at all, then he did so during the early to mid-nineteenth century. During this time numerous wars were fought between Turkey and Russia, including the Crimean War, and it is known that Russian prisoners were sometimes sent to the Ürgüp area. Moreover, it is noticeable that the stories of St John's miracles do not start to appear until about the 1830's.

The whole tradition is, of course, full of flaws. Embalmed bodies do not just disappear, and yet no one knows where it went to. And several more large question-marks remain—the church which was supposedly built in the 1890's now no longer exists, so where has it gone, and why can nobody in Ürgüp even vaguely recall its existence? One clue may lie in the recesses of the Russian monasteries on Mount Athos, where innumerable relics probably lie forgotten among the quarters of the few remaining monks. Does the hand of St John the Russian lie there? And yet, even if it does not, the story of St John is still worth repeating, for it must presumably be based on *something*—legends do not simply appear, even if the story of St John is baffling.

Then there occurred in 1908 the most baffling episode of all. In that year Ürgüp suffered a cholera epidemic which affected in particular the children in the Turkish quarter. The Turks, who apparently now also respected the body of St John, asked the

Orthodox population for permission to pray to St John for help. The Christians agreed to this, and the embalmed body was subsequently paraded through the streets of the Turkish part, carefully mounted on an expensive bier. Moslems apparently thronged the street as it passed; women are said to have thrown precious embroidered handkerchiefs on to the passing coffin, and even men wept with emotion. Not unexpectedly, the epidemic stopped a short time later. And with that, the last of St John the Russian's miracles seem to have been performed, for thereafter, all mention of the saint ceases abruptly. . . .

I first came across the story while browsing in the library of the British Archaeological Institute in Ankara, though I have since found the tale mentioned in a few more dusty books. But the strange thing is that no one in Ürgüp remembers the events of 1908, and there are no remains of the church. St John the Russian, of Ürgüp, remains an enigma.

The following day we set off early for Göreme. As usual the sun was up long before we were, and the day was already very warm as we piled into the oven-hot car, winced on the superheated plastic seating, and set off for the Göreme car-park. There we wandered around the churches at leisure, sometimes climbing up well-worn steps to reach inaccessible windows, and invariably returning to ground level rather disappointed—all churches worth visiting had been signposted, and could easily be reached. We drove on through Avcilar and I waved to the old man who had once hired me his donkeys. Ignoring the climb up to Uchişar, we took the long dust road to Avanos—the road where I had earlier met the little old lady who sang to herself. There were two villages on this road, and we decided to visit them both.

Çavuşin, the first village, lay about half a mile from the main track to Avanos. At the turning we discovered two more churches close to which was a drinking well, where herd-boys came to water their scraggy cattle and flocks of dusty goats and sheep. We passed a few droopy animals and a boy, curled up in the shade of a giant sheep-dog, and I saw the dog look up lazily as we bumped off down the rutted track towards the flat roofs of Çavuşin.

We found the village nestling under an awesome overhang of much-eroded and tunnelled tufa rock, glowing deep honey colour in the morning sunshine. This cliff had obviously housed the original community, for an interesting church survived half-way up, its few remaining columns still clinging to the crumbling precipice. To inspect this chapel we had to clamber over fallen boulders and slither through several narrow tunnels, but once among those perilously-balanced columns the rewards were great. The church's windows were decorated with stone carved bandeaux in what seemed to be a foreign style: I later learned that these mouldings were in fact of the Syrian type to be seen in the ruined monastery of Qala'at Saman, so I was rather pleased to to have recognised further foreign influences at work in Cappadocia!

The rest of the village huddled below these columns in a cluster round the mosque, though as in Ortahisar there was also a newer housing quarter further off, where the sun glanced and sparkled off a patchwork of pink and blue painted walls. A crowd of curious children watched us descend again to village level until a group of old men, sitting under a trelliswork of vines in the garden of the mosque, told them to be more polite to strangers. But the children didn't listen, and as we stumbled back on to the main street, they crowded around and followed us everywhere.

The children soon realised that we wanted to explore their village, and in no time they were arguing among themselves as to what to show us. Eventually they reached a consensus of opinion and with great eagerness directed our attention to an insignificant little rock-cut house not a dozen yards from the mosque. We entered and found ourselves in a strange old mill, for the house consisted of a single room, largely occupied by a colossal mill-stone placed like a central table. A wooden spindle created a vertical shaft, and into this a pole-like lever had been inserted so that the mill-stone could be turned by a donkey, or a miller, like sailors handling a capstan. The little boys immediately began to fool around, trying hard to push the lever so as to turn the wheel, but they were too weak and eventually they gave up, rather embarrassed by their failure to impress us.

Suddenly I noticed that the mill was vaulted, and as I began to study the grimy black ceiling, I also began to make out faint crosses carved into the arches. Had this been a Christian mill at one time, or was this yet another dilapidated church, now used by the Turks as a mill? I felt, on balance, that it had probably been a church . . . which was a pity, for it would have been exciting to have stumbled upon a Byzantine flour mill still in operation.

We eventually bumped back down the donkey-track past the herdsboy still sleeping in the shade of his dog, and turning right, continued on our way towards Avanos. We had another visit to make before reaching the Kizilirmak river, however, for a sign-post pointed to the village of Zilve, and we duly turned off the main track once more and headed for this unusual hamlet.

Zilve was the area's only underground Turkish community: whereas in Ortahisar and Çavuşin we had seen old rock-cut homes now being used as storage sheds, even the innermost rooms of homes built into the rock, we had never seen anything quite like Zilve, where the entire community lived in an impenetrable honeycomb of caves and rock-cut tunnels. There was even an underground mosque, its simple little *ciborium* jutting out of the rock like a weird chimney. How strange it must have been—a muezzin calling his faithful to worship in a valley which for so many centuries was the secret sanctuary of Orthodoxy!

Zilve was surely one of the best-hidden villages in Turkey. Even reaching it involved travelling down a long lateral valley, which wound and twisted through amazing forests of rock peaks until the scrubby plains and further-off cones of Göreme were long out of sight. At the head of this valley lay the village—not that we realised it—for the entire community was completely hidden underground. Because of its relative underdevelopment as a tourist site, there were hardly any windows, no signposts, nothing—only a few tracks leading off into the jumble of rocks which marked the end of the valley. (In later visits I found that a tea-house had since been built. Its owner now charged a small fee for access into the village—such is progress.)

We left the car and began our explorations. The site had once clearly been a Christian village, for we discovered at least two very dilapidated chapels, with faded paintings and broken-down interiors. But the more we wandered around, the more we began to feel that the site must have been occupied until modern times: steps had been cut quite recently in places, and the strange little mosque also indicated recent habitation in Zilve—all very puzzling.

Fortunately we were joined by a local farmer who had been attracted to our party by our exclamations. According to this fellow, the village of Zilve had originally been a Christian community, but was abandoned by the Greeks in the fourteenth century when the main centre at Göreme went out of use. The village was subsequently occupied by local Turks (he didn't know when), and in fact these Turks continued to live in their village until the early 1950's, when it was felt by the Turkish government that their conditions of existence had become too primitive and insanitary, and when the population was forcibly ejected from their soot-encrusted caves, and moved to a new village called Yeni Zilve, a couple of miles away. So the strange site became a ghost town, soon to be strewn with tumbleweed and scrub. Its mosque was now barren, its tunnels were now black and fathomless.

Eventually we left this shanty village and headed back down its protective valley towards the road to Avanos, wondering how old folk and cripples, babies and sick people, could have managed to climb the steep rock-cut steps which so often were the only access to many of Zilve's homes. To think of people living in caves in the technological age of the twentieth century was somehow more jolting than imagining long-forgotten monks doing so.

At the point where the Zilve track joined the main path to Avanos, there stood a long outcrop of multi-stratified tufa rock, rather like those huge masas and butes which appear in cowboy films. A few lonely fingers of rock pointed skywards, stranded from the main bute like the Isle of Wight's Needles, and to my surprise Mr Frandsen pulled the car up by one of these fingers.

'We can have lunch now,' he said, and to my amazement the Danes began unloading an entire picnic from the boot of their car, and soon we were sitting in the shade of that rocky cone, a fire briskly heating up coffee while all sorts of foodstuffs were unwrapped from tinfoil packs. It was wonderful . . . smorgasbord, sardines, Danish butter, even bacon. How I longed for bacon! I had long learned that in Moslem Turkey, bacon could not be found—so imagine my delight when we had bacon sandwiches in the private shade of our rocky spire.

Having cleared away with typical Danish cleanliness, we set off in the car once more—but not to Avanos, for Mr Frandsen said he would now take me to see the 'underground cities' of Kaymakli and Derinkuyu, in return for my having guided his party all morning. We sped westwards, passing the towers of Uçhisar, and soon we could see Nevşehir's little Seljuk castle. We then turned off at the town's hospital and were soon heading south towards the town of Niğde. Our road was virtually dead straight, and I recalled that it had been built by Justinian as a military counter against the Arabs, though his system of new roads, beacons, and fortresses, actually proved of little use against the lightning raids of those Moslem horsemen.

The scenery was incredibly bleak. To the west lay the barren Melendiz hills, where so many early Christians had once sought refuge as hermits. To the east stretched the plains of Cappadocia, flat and endless, broken only by the snowy peak of Mount Erciyas in the distance. And ahead of us lay the village of Kaymakli, a few drab brown sun-baked houses straggling round the central square. We slowed down to avoid the crowd of children who came to inspect our car, and, turning off the main road, bumped to a halt outside an inconspicuous little rock-cut door. Here we were greeted by a friendly fellow who introduced himself as Mustafa Agar, the guide to Kaymakli's 'underground city'. We followed him through a rock-cut door, noted an immediate chill in the air, and duly set off in single file down into the bowels of this strange, weird 'underground city'.

No book has yet detailed the underground refuges of Cappadocia, for their history has been very difficult to ascertain, but it seems likely that they were constructed by Christians during the second and third centuries in order to escape persecution, possibly from the Romans (who were still pagans), possibly from marauding Persians. What *is* clear is that, under conditions of extreme danger, these Christians scraped and chiselled the most incredible underground systems of tunnels and chambers to be seen in Turkey . . . and the best example so far discovered lies under the village of Kaymakli. This 'underground city', as it has come to be called, descends to a depth of about three hundred feet by a series of chambers and inter-connected tunnels, on some seven different floors or levels. Each floor had a communal kitchen, a chapel, and extensive family accommodation, and there is also evidence of an underground hospital, several tombs, a system of wind-shafts, and many storage rooms.

This entire catacomb-like structure now extends below Kaymakli, once a Christian community close to the safety of the Melendiz hills. Its full underground area has not yet been properly explored, for even today villagers are hesitant about entering some of the deeper tunnels. It is at least several square miles, however, indicating that in times of crisis, this 'underground city' must have been capable of housing a great many people, possibly numbering thousands: these people normally lived in the small village above the site, and would only have retired into the tunnels as a means of escaping from persecution. The uppermost tunnels and rooms were probably used as permanent stables and storehouses, for not only were they handy as byres and granaries, but the cool atmosphere of the tunnels was also a good food preservative. By thus using the tunnels nearest the surface, food supplies for a lengthy stay underground were immediately available, in the event of sudden attack.

The villagers clearly relied on two main factors for defence: one was that enemies could only remain in the district for as long as they had food and water, and since most food was stored underground, soldiers would therefore not be able to stay in the bleak surroundings of Kaymakli for long; secondly, huge round stone wheels were rolled from side niches across all entrance tunnels as soon as everyone was inside. These wheels were so big, and the passages so narrow, that it was impossible to get past them. In some cases loop tunnels were made round them, perhaps by enemies trying to reach the Christians beyond, but there were always more wheels further on. These wheels sometimes had small holes bored in them, which enabled the Christians to keep a look-out on enemy activities. Thus people could live longer underground than could their attackers above them. Moreover, intruders could not even smoke the Christians out of their holes, as happened elsewhere in the Middle East, for Kaymakli had a number of wind-shafts which descended right down to the deepest levels of the refuge, and whose surface holes were always cleverly disguised. Since these were probably only opened at night, enemies probably never discovered how to prevent the tunnels from getting air.

Life for the Christians, when forced into their catacombs, was no joke. Their villages and fields were inevitably destroyed while they remained helpless underground, unable to prevent enemies looting as they pleased. Living quarters were cramped and uncomfortable, and since only the largest communal rooms had any headroom, people had generally to stoop all the time. Intercommunicating tunnels were narrow and badly lit, and the entire structure was, of course, very stuffy because of the continual need for burning torches and cooking hearths. Lighting was by torches inserted into wall notches, and kitchen fires were burned where convenient—since there were no flues, the walls of the catacombs also became covered with thick grimy layers of soot.

Living quarters consisted simply of square rooms containing only the barest essentials for a family—beds, for example, were usually only rough shelves carved into the solid rock. Apart from a few primitive crosses etched out on the walls of the chapels, there was little decoration or artistic expression.

Furthermore, it was always night in these tunnels, and while soldiers remained above them, babies, sick folk and old people saw no sunshine, had no fresh air, and drank no fresh water. Illness was probably always rampant because of the lack of sanitation and the forced restricted diet; the conditions of communal life helped also to spread infectious diseases, which probably then caused epidemics. Corpses also had to remain underground until they could be properly buried on the surface, for cremation was not practised.

Food consisted of whatever the Christians had time to carry into the tunnels when warned of approaching enemies. No one knows if there was an underground well at Kaymakli, but there was one at a second refuge below the village of Derinkuyu, five miles away; these two sites were linked by a tunnel through which men could have passed with water pitchers. The Christians also had primitive underground wine presses, with shallow basins in which they trod grapes, and huge vats in which they stored the fermenting liquid. They also had ovens, probably for making bread, but these were used sparingly because of the lack of fuel—Cappadocia's lack of trees probably meant that dung was used where possible.

Vegetables were probably rare, but fruits such as apples and pears were probably quite common, providing much-needed vitamins during long spells underground. The underground cells were, in fact, particularly ideal for the preservation of fruit. (In some Cappadocian villages today, caves are still used to preserve lemons and grapefruit.)

The most extraordinary aspect of the underground refuges, however, lies in their very creation. Their sizes are phenomenal and the work involved must have taken years of patient chiselling and scraping. Unfortunately, the names of the masons are unknown, for no written evidence survives, nor is it even clear how many people these strange sites held. Villages in those days were not big, and yet there seems to have been room for many refugees—estimates vary from one thousand to as much as thirty thousand, which only proves that it is impossible to tell for certain how many people used Kaymakli.

And there remains yet another mystery. There are miles of tunnels and chambers, storage rooms and wind-shafts, but there is no trace whatever of the rubble which must have been excavated as the result of digging. Some may have been used in the construction of village houses and field walls, but this would account for very little . . . and no one knows where the rest went.

We re-emerged from the darkness of the tunnels, and blinked in the fierce sunlight.

'You like my underground city?' inquired Mustafa, our fearless guide.

We all laughed. 'Of course!' I replied, 'But tell me, how long have people been coming here to see your tunnels?'

Mustafa smiled. 'You are not the first, I am sorry. But the tunnels were opened only in 1964, which is not so long ago. Before then it was very dangerous, for there was no electric light, and there was no guide. We had to warn our children about the tunnels, for it was very easy to get lost in the darkness. And if people wanted to look for valuable things deep in the city, they had to fill their pockets with grass—then they made a trail to follow when they wanted to find the door again.

'But now we have the electric system, and I am a guide, and so it is easier. But we must still be careful, for it is possible to become trapped if some rocks fall, and also there are very many parts of the tunnels which we do not visit because they are broken. But when Mustafa is the guide, everything is easy!'

We all laughed, pressed a few lira into his hopeful hand, and climbed back into the car again. Waving to the beaming Mustafa, we bumped off back to the main road and set off for the next village to see the second underground city. As we jolted through the streets towards the main road, some children stoned the car, which was dented. It was the first time I had seen tourists being stoned in Turkey.

The hamlet of Derinkuyu seemed to be almost a replica of Kaymakli, except that it was dominated by two imposing Orthodox styled buildings, both of which had obviously been churches. The village had therefore been once a Greek community, and since a Greek inscription on one church was dated 1858, we assumed that this had been an Orthodox settlement until the exchanges of population in 1923. This renewed our interest in the underground tunnels, for surely very few Anatolian villages could boast of evidence covering both the earliest and more recent eras in Christian history?

The underground tunnels seemed older than those which we had inspected in Kaymakli, but in essence they were the same, save that the rock had been cut and excavated more roughly. There were also a number of steps where in Kaymakli there had only been steep slopes, and at the lowest point where visitors could go, someone had built a simple rest room with tables and chairs, but regrettably no tea-house. A glass of hot tea would have been welcome in the chilly depths of the tunnels. It did not take us long to see the city, and as we reappeared outside, my only regret was that we had not been able to find Derinkuyu's well, said to have provided water for the people holed up in Kaymakli. One of my ambitions now is to find that well, and to carry water along that five-mile tunnel to Kaymakli.

We then set off to examine the two churches. One at the far end of the village was open, and a crowd of curious youngsters watched us enter. It was as if we had stepped into a different world, for as we opened the church door, we found ourselves standing quite unexpectedly in . . . a cement factory! A ghastly sinking feeling overcame us, and sadly we set out to discover if anything Greek still survived in this disappointing place, meanwhile under the curious gaze of cement workers all uniformly covered in a drab grey dust. A sorry *Christus* looked down from a central dome, from which hung a loose chain that had obviously once supported a wrought-iron chandelier. A few columns retained their painted decorations below layers of cement dust, and a dilapidated pulpit was now used by the workers as an observation platform above the throbbing machinery now assembled in the nave and aisles. A locked door, painted with an explicit skull and jagged lightning, barred entry into the vestry. And almost thankfully, we left this sad place and went off to the other Greek building which, because it now supported an additional minaret, we assumed was now a mosque.

The mosque was surprisingly locked when we arrived, but as

Dolmabahçe Palace from the waterfront

Istanbul's Rumeli Hisar with the Bosphorus beyond

Sherbet water seller in Istanbul

Ara displays a carpet to a visiting tourist

we were about to leave the *hoca* appeared and with a polite smile he let us in. The interior was, thankfully, in stark contrast to the unfortunate church at the other end of the village; almost amazingly, Greek paintings survived, and in fact seemed actually to have been restored. Indeed the general decor of the mosque was strongly reminiscent of a church, save for the addition of various pieces of Islamic furniture.

It turned out that the church, on its abandonment by the Greeks in the 1920's, had been earmarked for demolition, but the village raised enough money to have the five-hundred-year-old (or so I was told) building preserved, saying that they would convert it into a mosque. Miraculously, the Christian paintings in the interior were also carefully preserved and incorporated into the decor of the new mosque—a unique concession to the representation of living beings, for Islam forbids the drawing of life in religious art. So portraits of apostles and martyrs happily survived in this unusual mosque. The church's rood used to incorporate a screen on which were thirty-three panels illustrating events in the life of Jesus, and even this screen remained except that the panels had been replaced by thirty-three passages from the Koran.

We left the mosque, our spirits revived once more after the discovery of the cement works, and together with the *hoca*, we went to the local tea-house for a drink. Seated around a table, the conversation turned to comparative religions. We found our village priest surprisingly broadminded, and he seemed to enjoy talking of the many points of belief shared by Islam and Christianity. As we left him, I felt really quite uplifted, though drained mentally from having had so much difficult translation to do! And as we drove out of Derinkuyu, with the *hoca* standing in the dusty street waving to our departing car, a cluster of curious villagers smiled at this happy meeting of East and West.

I thought of St John the Russian, and the Mohammedans of Ürgüp who had believed in his miraculous powers. I remembered the little rock-cut mosque at Zilve where Turkish villagers lived after the Christians had gone. And I thought happily of the mosque at Derinkuyu, where the villagers had preserved the lovely Greek paintings in an old Orthodox church. It had been a happy day, for I had, perhaps surprisingly, found a real bridge between East and West, not among the concrete and glass blocks of Istanbul, but here among the villagers of Anatolia, where life was still genuine and beliefs were sincere.

7 *Ramadan and Winter*

Somewhere around the middle of November, the first flakes of snow began to drift down from a leaden sky, and I knew that winter was now on its way. To the east, I could see the snowline on Mount Erciyas creeping daily down the mountain side, and from the Russian steppes, chilly biting winds began to sweep across the Anatolian Plateau, bringing with them wolves and frost—Ortahisar lay at almost the same altitude as the summit of Ben Nevis, Britain's highest mountain.

As the cold grew more intense, and the snow began to lie for days on end, I started to grow a beard. The villagers watched the slow growth of this beard for some time, saying nothing. I was aware of the fact that it was causing comment in the tea-houses and barber shops, but still nothing was said to me personally. People would stare at me as I walked about, and I could feel eyes watching me everywhere, but I could not understand the conspiracy of silence. Eventually I asked Tahir for the reason—were there not many men in the village with beards?

'You see,' he said kindly, 'the people here like you, and they do not want to offend you. But in Ortahisar, only the wise and the venerable old men have beards—and I'm afraid that you don't yet count as either of these!'

So, without my beard, I faced the oncome of winter. I had no real idea of what to expect, but had brought a heavy anorak with me should things prove to be worse than a British winter. At the same time the nights grew longer: with nothing much to do in the evenings except play endless backgammon with people in the tea-houses, I decided to start language lessons in the hotel. I explained to Yaşar bey, the mayor, that I thought it silly that I should be guiding visitors to Ortahisar, and that I wished to teach any willing students both the rudiments of English, French and German, and also the history and art of their own localities. He seemed delighted with the idea, and spread the word around, with the result that within a week I had assembled a group of about twelve boys, and classes began at once, three nights a week, in one of the now-deserted rooms in the inn. The boys were all pupils at the Middle School in Ürgüp, where they were also learning English, so they were all able to provide grammar text books, and with that we got down to studying.

I found that I had to be careful when explaining the history of Göreme to my pupils, for many did not like being told the history of their own area by a foreigner—this raised the problem of 'loss of face', which all Turks dislike. I also took some time in adjusting to the speed with which my pupils were able to grasp their English, but eventually we were able to get past the stage of simply reading 'Mr Brown and Mrs Brown and Jack and Jill are going to the cinema. Mrs Brown is wearing a green coat' . . . etc., and by December, my best pupils were actually able to say things like 'Göreme is a very interesting place. It has many churches. They are very old. There are many beautiful pictures (this was an easier word apparently than paintings) and they are also very old. . . .'

Basically, I explained the history and art of Göreme to my pupils in Turkish, so that they would at least understand it thoroughly. If they knew it well, then even should I fail to teach them much English or French, they would at least have the knowledge of their history stored away for another time. When trying to teach English, which I did before attempting any other languages, I concentrated on conversation, without too much regard for precise grammar so long as the essential meaning was clear—the grammar would no doubt be taught at Middle School. Thus my hope was to turn out pupils who both knew the history of Cappadocia well, and understood who the various figures were in most of the important paintings, but who could also convey this in some form of broken but understandable English to visitors. While I would not claim all that much success, for I had only until mid-December in which to achieve anything, I would at least claim that some of my pupils did well, and I could visualise a few of them doing modestly well when spring came round. And if nothing else, the language lessons did at least pass the long nights of winter.

One day, as Tahir and I sat passing another endless hour in backgammon and drinking tea on the tea-house balcony, my attention was distracted by the sight of an unshaven, skip-capped individual sitting at a corner table, and clearly in some pain. People were gathered round about, making it difficult to see what was happening, so we went over to investigate.

'It's old Hasan—he's got a bad tooth,' said someone. I pushed through the crowd to see if I could offer him any medicines, but it was only to discover that Hasan was in the process of having his tooth extracted by a pair of household pliers, wielded by one of his friends who was at that moment busy wrenching and pulling and tugging with such vigour that I could well understand why he was in such pain. Suddenly, with a yelp of triumph, the friend held aloft for all to see, a tooth with a dreadful cavity, while old Hasan gave a weak smile of gratitude. He had clearly suffered during this crude extraction, but as a man he was apparently determined not to show this, just as his friends simply went back to their backgammon boards, obviously expecting him to make no further comment either. Only Mustafa, the owner of the tea-house, showed any sympathy, and offered Hasan a free glass of tea for a mouthwash and a hookah pipe for a good smoke. In a moment the incident had been forgotten, and the tooth lay discarded on the floor.

With the onset of winter, I found myself absorbing every detail of these occasional incidents, for I lacked the ability just to sit and do nothing all day, as the men seemed able to do. I now pounced upon the slightest variation to the day, noticing every sight and sound as if I had never seen them before—such was the boredom generated by Ortahisar's winter. In fact I was amazed by the wealth of detail in village life which I now suddenly began to see: the iron welder at work on an old bedstead, a starving chicken, even the depth of snow on the flat roofs of the houses.

A few days later it was December, and with it came Ramadan. It so happened that this festival occurred in winter, though it could have been any time, for it moves backwards ten days each year. Ramadan, I soon learned, was the Mohammedan month of fasting, when no one was allowed to eat, smoke, or drink during the day, which was officially ended each evening at five o'clock by the wailing minaret. Only the very elderly, the chronically sick, and babies were excepted—which meant that I was faced with the problem of whether to join Ortahisar's villagers, or eat privately in my hotel room.

I accepted Ramadan as a challenge, though I actually had little choice, for every village shop was closed until five in the evening, as were the restaurant and tea-houses—people were free to play backgammon and dominoes, but until five there was never any sign of tea or hookah pipes. Like everyone else, I now took to backgammon in earnest, for with inches of permanent snow lying all around, what else was there to do? Farming was at a standstill, tourists had all long disappeared, and with no food to give me energy, I did not feel inclined to go tramping round snow-bound Göreme. Backgammon was all that was left. Although I played with many villagers, I spent most of my time with Tahir, aimlessly tossing dice and shuffling the plastic backgammon discs for hours. It was an incredibly tedious way to pass a day.

The approach of evening brought new interest, however, for during the last few minutes before the wailing of the muezzin at five o'clock, people would begin to drift, almost surreptitiously, into the tea-houses, carrying with them strange paper parcels. At about four minutes to five, these packets would be unwrapped to reveal bread and cheese and olives, while Mustafa the tea-house owner might be seen stoking up the fire for his samovar. With two minutes to go, people might be seen actually smacking their lips and casting anxious glances at ponderous pocket watches. At one minute to five, Mustafa would be waiting poised with a tray of steaming glasses of tea, and every villager would be seated, anxiously listening for the minaret's first notes. Ortahisar's muezzin still preferred to sing without the aid of a microphone on important days, so everyone would be waiting with strained ears for his first wavering wail. And as soon as that initial cry was heard, Mustafa would be rushing off round the tables with his tray, hookah pipes would be bubbling away, and scores of tea glasses would be tinkling to the stirring of tiny teaspoons. Backgammon boards would lie forgotten as villagers tucked busily into their bread and cheese meals, and in seconds the sleepy, bored tea-house would have been transformed into a busy, noisy rogue's den once again, just like any normal day. Meanwhile, shops outside would be removing their shutters, and in scores of homes, village women would be completing their private prayers, and cooking meals for their children.

Following this orgy of eating, most people went to bed, to sleep off the bloated feeling of gluttony. Because of the need to feed again before daybreak, however, Ortahisar employed its musicians to wake people up again in time for a second meal. Ortahisar's 'band' actually consisted of only a clarinet player and a fellow who clattered a bass drum slung round his shoulder, played by thumping one deep-sounding side with a heavy stick, while rat-tat-tatting on the other tighter skin with a thin twig. The end effect was like the entire drum section of a Scottish pipe band. Like many Turkish instruments, I discovered that to play this drum was deceptively difficult.

The clarinet player and drummer were, therefore, employed during Ramadan to perform throughout the entire village in good time to waken everyone up before sunrise. It took some time to accustom myself to their distant bangings and wailings at three o'clock each wintry December morning, but in time I grew used to them, and I would sleepily join Tahir for a meal before the morning minaret call. As I walked through the village each morning to Tahir's house, I would see lights coming on here and there as people lit their oil lamps; and as the musicians wandered through each quarter of the village, so more and more little pin-pricks of light would appear as Ortahisar woke to face another long dreary day, waiting for the evening minaret call—it was rather a beautiful sight in the snowy light of early morning. And then as Tahir and I tucked into our last food before evening, I would remember that throughout the entire world of Islam, people would be doing likewise.

I suppose that had Ramadan occurred at any other time of the year, I would still have had plenty to do—harvests always have to be collected, apple trees tended, sheep herded into market, or tourists guided round Göreme—but in winter, the combination of Ramadan and snow brought the entire village to a total halt, and, save for the traditional carpet weaving, complete inactivity descended on Ortahisar. Sometimes I hung around Mustafa's tea-house, playing dominoes and backgammon, and occasionally I retired to my room in the deserted inn, where I typed and tried to keep warm. I was given a tiny stove—a sorry affair manufactured from an oversize tin can, connected to the outside world by a rickety chimney of smaller cans soldered together and pushed through a hole in the wall. I used to burn furniture in this stove, but eventually the inn ran out of firewood, and I started on an enormous pile of *Sunday Times* newspapers, which I had been receiving from home in an effort to keep up to date with world events. Strangely enough, I suddenly found myself with plenty to do, for I now began rereading all my favourite articles before finally condemning them to my fiery furnace.

I also learned to frizzle apple slices on my stove. The village mayor used to leave a whole pannier of apples outside my door each week, but there were always so many apples left by the time the next load arrived that I had to devise ways of varying their presentation when eating them. I tried various ways, but eventually I decided that, so long as I ignored the paint and solder which stuck to the roasted undersides of my apple slices, they were most appetising when frizzled on the lid of my hot tin stove. But alas, the bottom finally dropped off the stove, and realising that I would now have no heat, nor any frizzled apples, I decided to leave Ortahisar to its last ten days of Ramadan and the rest of its chilly winter, and to return to Istanbul, where I hoped it would be less cold.

I soon discovered that, while it was easy to decide to go to Istanbul, it was virtually impossible to find any bus prepared to make the hazardous journey through the snow. Eventually I was able to catch a bus prepared to go as far as Ankara, and so in the early morning we set off into the winter, first to Nevşehir where people huddled around trying to keep warm, and then up into the hills beyond.

The outstanding feature of this bus was what we were proud to describe as its heating system. This magnificent achievement of engineering consisted of a baby's chamber pot, filled with glowing charcoals! Although this gave off an agreeable heat, the only trouble was that it could only be in one part of the bus at any one time, so if it was in the aisle at the front, the people at the back would set up a loud chorus of complaints, while if it was at the back passengers at the front would protest instead, sometimes even forcing the driver to stop until they got the potty back again! Wherever it was, the traditional thing to do, apparently, was to take off your socks and shoes and warm your feet over the rising heat—but the smell of all those steaming feet was awful! It was useless to complain, however, so I took off my socks too, and steamed along with everyone else.

We had not long left Nevşehir when, with a loud splutter, our bus's engine stopped, and we coasted to a gentle halt in the middle of nowhere, surrounded by snow and threatening hills with not a house in sight. With much cursing and muttering, the driver disappeared to check the motor, and the passengers fell into desultory conversation. Half an hour later, however, the driver had not yet reappeared, and a crowd of angry passengers went off to see what he was up to. Tapping the shivering, oil-bespattered fellow on the shoulder, they pulled him off the engine cowl and replaced him with one of their number who claimed to be a part-time mechanic in some remote country garage. So once again, we all fell into hum-drum conversation inside the bus, while the driver looked anxiously out of the window, clearly worried about what was happening to his precious motor. Time passed, the potty was stoked up again, the smell of feet became almost intolerable, and eventually another bus passed by, with much hooting on its horns and laughter from its passengers. As a result a noisy deputation went back to the bonnet—where an amazing sight greeted their eyes. The village mechanic had dismantled every single moving part of the engine, and had laid all the components out in neat rows in the snow! It was a most extraordinary exhibition, but clearly it was not going to help us, so the mechanic was dismissed, and the leader of the grumblers, who was only a tailor, took over, while we returned to the bus and waited once more. By now the poor driver was on the brink of despair as he watched his bus's engine being disembowelled by amateurs, but eventually the tailor returned, after much tinkering. Miraculously the engine sparked into life at the first attempt, and with great satisfaction, he sat himself down on the back seat and demanded the potty.

Ankara looked grey and dull as we arrived, hours late. People seemed to slouch around the streets, their collars turned up against the plateau's icy winds. Eventually I found another bus willing to try for Istanbul, and as evening fell, we set off into the snow once more. All night long we shivered and huddled, and twice the bus broke down in the darkness, forcing the driver to look for assistance on both occasions. The second time he seemed to have been away for ages, and people were beginning to wonder what had happened to him, when he suddenly reappeared, covered in frozen snow and looking a courageous but pitiful sight.

Morning found us bitterly cold but at least still moving, which, as the dawn became more transparent, seemed to be more than other vehicles could manage. All around us, abandoned lorries and vans lay littered in grotesque positions, and in the depths of one snowy gully I saw the charred wreckage of another unfortunate car. Slowly we crawled over the Pontic mountains, thanking the driver in our hearts for having fitted snow chains on to the wheels at some time during the night. All around us, vehicles were slipping and skidding and slithering backwards down the slopes, but we crept on, slowly but safely. For hours we maintained this slow walking pace, through intermittent snow falls and a howling wind. We passed groups of people stamping and waving their arms in the snow to keep warm, and somewhere around Adapazari we passed a bus which was on fire. Then at last we reached the short stretch of motorway which heralded the approach to Haydarpasha and the Bosphorus, and thankfully I disembarked, glad to have survived that carnage of wrecked and abandoned cars.

I reached Bostanci and the Algan house exhausted and bitterly cold. Although I had been unable to warn Mrs Algan of my impending arrival, she seemed delighted to see me. A welcome meal was immediately provided, and I was shown to the room which would be mine until the spring. Everybody seemed happy at my return: Nezih soon was showing off the latest English phrases which he had learned at school, Şefik *baba* produced a bottle of raki and toasted my arrival, while all three daughters worked busily in the kitchen.

There was not yet any snow in Bostanci, but a chilly wind meant that the threat was always imminent, and so dinner consisted of lovely warm lentil soup, followed by grilled meatballs, chops, stuffed peppers and tomatoes, aubergines, carrots, artichokes and roast potatoes, chased by piles of newly-baked cheese and mince *böreks*, all laced with Mrs Algan's secret savoury recipe—delicious! I felt rather pleased to be missing Ortahisar's rather spartan potato soup and beans! And then, once the coffee had been drunk and we had danced much of the night away in a flurry of finger-snapping and beads of perspiration, we joined Ortahisar in going to bed. Only this time there would be no drummer and no wailing clarinet to waken me in the early hours of morning. For the first time in twenty days, I was able to sleep peacefully, confident that when I awoke I would be able, at last, to enjoy another breakfast.

In fact, Granny Algan did observe Ramadan, and even Nezih and his father went to the local mosque to attend morning service, but these apart, I was told that the Algans did not bother much with fasting. Indeed most of Istanbul seemed to be unconcerned by Ramadan—perhaps because people had still to work in offices and shops throughout the day. As I set off the next day to visit Mehmet Ali at the bazaar, I passed countless busy restaurants, and almost every food shop was open too, crowded with housewives as on any other day. Then suddenly I realised that in Britain the shops would also be crowded, but with people buying up for Christmas, and for the first time since my arrival in Turkey several months earlier, I felt homesick.

8 *Bazaars and Betrothals*

I found Mehmet Ali sitting disconsolately outside his shop, but as I approached he jumped up happily and pumped my hand as if I were his long-lost friend. At least I could understand his babbling Turkish now, and as tea arrived we sat down and talked of the summer's tourist business. Times had been good, he said, but in the bazaar world, so much could depend on outside factors. Cruise ships calling at Istanbul could be diverted by political unrest or disease, but the summer had been a good one, and Ara had sold many carpets. Now there was no business to cajole into the shop, however, and slowly Mehmet Ali's happiness had subsided into the routine and boredom of day-to-day sitting around.

Nevertheless, he agreed to take me on as an apprentice carpet seller, especially since I could speak Dutch, one of the few languages unknown to Ara. Over a final glass of tea for the day, Ara promised to teach me all about carpets during the winter months, and should tourists pass by, I would be expected to do my share of selling. Sadly, the uncertain weather meant that I might be unable to reach the Bazaar every day, for Istanbul's winter had become just as bad as Ortahisar's and the journey from Bostanci to the Bosphorus was becoming increasingly prone to snow blockages. But I promised Mehmet Ali to be present whenever possible.

Christmas soon arrived, but really it seemed like any other day in the Moslem household of the Algans—there were no decorations, no lights, and there was no tree. I had only a few Christmas cards, which looked down sadly from my bedroom mantelpiece—my only remainders of the festive season. . . . But then that evening, a beaming Selma *anne* produced a beautifully cooked turkey, glistening golden brown and decorated with vegetables carefully arranged around the perimeter of the serving dish.

'I think you eat turkey in England . . .' she said, presenting me with the carving knife, and with a sudden big lump in my throat

I began to cut, to a chorus of 'Happy Noels!' from the assembled, happy family. Afterwards, there was dancing and laughter into the small hours. And when I finally went to bed, I found a little package lying waiting for me, with a label which read: 'To Craig, from Nezih, Happy Noels'. So I had my Christmas after all.

On Boxing Day we awoke to find Bostanci completely isolated by blocked roads, and for some days it was impossible to reach the city. Our water, and periodically the electricity, were cut off, and soon neighbouring families began clubbing together when attempting to fetch from the local shops. Even when it *was* possible to reach the shops, we usually found that there was a shortage of essentials like bread and milk.

While thus stranded in Bostanci, I was invited to join some local boys in the formation of a 'beat' group, and we spent our snow-bound days rehearsing for coming appearances. Our group, called the 'Shining Lights', consisted of a drummer, organist, and three guitars—I sang English hit songs and played rhythm guitar. Eventually we sallied forth to perform at local dances, where we soon became established as a popular dance band, capable of playing both Turkish and Western music. Very soon we were offered a contract to play at an American-frequented night-club in the small town of Ereğli.

Our hire was for the duration of the New Year and Ramadan celebrations. It happened that Ramadan ended that year on 1st January, which, like the end of every Ramadan, had to be marked with three days of celebration. It was therefore a simple matter to hire us for New Year's Eve, plus the following three days of festivity, and we duly signed for the four-day contract.

Reaching Ereğli, a small town stranded on the inhospitable Black Sea coast, and hemmed into the shore by high, snowy mountains, was not so easy. Eventually we persuaded a dolmuş mini-bus to transport us, for a fare of about £15, to this cut-off township, and after slithering and skidding through slush and snow for an entire afternoon and night, we finally pulled into its market-waterfront in the early hours of morning. Our first discovery was that our employers could offer us no accommodation, and sadly we made for a local hotel to spend the remainder of the night. Having crossed the Pontic mountains in the dark and along mud tracks, and having travelled by the coastal road—often little more than the beach itself—picking out holes and rocks on the track with flickering headlamps, we hardly relished having to spend some of the money which we had not yet earned.

But this was only the start of our trouble. Our employer broke his contract by not paying the fee promised, and by asking us to play longer than originally planned, but we enjoyed our music and so we played on . . . and on . . . and on. Midnight on New Year's Eve found us half-way through a cosy medley when, with cries of laughter and surprise, all the lights went out and twelve o'clock struck—leaving us playing on until our medley finished at ten past twelve. Then I thought of home, where Hogmanay would by then have been in full swing, and sadly I raised my glass of cheap local wine.

Then, once the adults had gone, we went on playing until daytime, and not a single teenager left the club until then—so it went on, enjoyably, for the next four days. I eventually contracted laryngitis, however, and decided to leave Ereğli earlier than the others.

I took an early morning bus—one of the few that was going to try to cross the mountains in winter—and we set off with the best wishes of most of the village, assembled in the market square to watch us leave. The town looked deceptively peaceful as we pulled out along the rutted coast road. The Black Sea gently lapped the harbour sands under a pink sky, and offshore a few ships rode quietly at anchor on a sea of glass. No casual observer could ever have guessed from such a tranquil scene that only a couple of miles inland terrible snow storms were raging through the Pontic mountains. I glanced at the village's vast and ugly American-supervised industrial complex which had brought prosperity to the small commercial backwater of Ereğli. One day, perhaps that prosperity would also be used to improve the dreadful road which connected the town to the outside world. In the meantime, our bus would fight its way through the mountains as best it could.

I arrived back in Istanbul to find the newspaper headlines

packed with descriptions of Turkey's unusually severe winter. A small Bosphorus ferry had capsized in strong gales with the loss of several lives. Daily press photographs illustrated weather conditions in other parts of Turkey—Malatya snowed up, Izmir under snow, Erzurum under many feet of drifts, Kars virtually cut off, with the police there desperately trying to rescue abandoned villagers from freezing to death. One photo brought comfort—it showed a curvy girl lying sunbathing on an Antalya beach, under the comment that the south coast never seemed to suffer from the cold like the rest of Asia Minor. But the next day Antalya experienced its first snow in living memory.

During this period of enforced inactivity, I learned a lot about family life Istanbul style—and yet in many ways also Ortahisar style. Although I had apparently been accepted into the family as another member, I nevertheless found myself being carefully treated as a guest, in spite of attempts to disguise this: arguments were always hushed up, I was never allowed to do anything for myself, and I was frequently presented with glasses of tea, and offers of 'please sit down', which only a guest would have received. Restrictions also appeared in human relationships—I was, for example, never allowed out in public with Merih, the youngest Algan daughter. Even Merih agreed that it would not have been fitting for me to be seen alone with her. Similarly, I was expected to spend my evenings playing cards or dominoes with the family's men-folk, leaving the women to their own chatter. And when with the men, I was always expected to drink my raki, and to hold my end up in domino-playing successfully. Sometimes I was challenged to feats of strength, and the men-folk would gather round to see who would win. It seemed that the only time the family ever came together was to listen to a few songs on the guitar, or to hear the children rendering 'Frère Jacques' in a variety of languages—a party-piece which I taught them during the worst of winter.

The house boasted a stove similar to my old tin-can affair at Ortahisar, but this one had fortunately been constructed from cast iron. Only the chimney, which meandered through the kitchen and dining room before disappearing through a hole in the outer wall, was made of tin sections. Otherwise, the house could have been European. The furniture was Western in taste—there were chairs and a sofa, in contrast to Ortahisar's carpet-covered divans and low round tables, where people sat on the floor. There was wallpaper and painted woodwork. Pictures replaced rugs on the walls, and a piano stood near the door. Thus, although the Algan house *looked* European, in its customs and traditions it still retained *something* of the Ottoman way of life.

Breakfast consisted of toast, cheese, olives, and tea. I had also the option of boiled eggs, but since I disliked eggs (most unfortunate for any traveller), I did without. Lunch usually meant soup, meat balls or chops, with vegetables such as aubergines, tomatoes or green beans, and rounded off with fruit salad or börek pastries—in effect a mixture of both Ottoman and Western influences once again. Indeed, the family's meals served only to confuse me further on what influences were the more dominant in this suburb of Istanbul—those of Islam or of Europe. In Ortahisar, tradition clearly still dominated the privacy of most homes, but it seemed that in Bostanci there was more of a dilemma. Architecturally, gastronomically, and in the ways people spent their leisure, there was a peculiar uncertainty of choice between the incoming ways of the West and the long-established ways of Islam and Ottoman Turkey.

As a village, Bostanci certainly boasted Western attractions and challenges—in warmer months a popular garden cinema played nightly to full houses, and throughout the year the 'Atlantik Sinema' attracted queues of mini-skirted girls and slick-suited youths, awaiting the appearance of Western film stars with great anticipation. Indeed, in Istanbul and its suburbs Western films were even preferable to Turkish ones—perhaps because of the city's greater acquaintance with English and Italian (spaghetti cowboy films were very popular), or perhaps because of a greater discrimination in quality. Anyway, this preference for Western films seemed to be yet another sign of the times, for city cinemas showing predominantly Turkish films seemed to be declining in number.

The people of Bostanci also *looked* more Westernised. There

Merih and myself after our betrothal

Ara, Mehmet Ali, and myself in the Bazaar

Copper craftsman working near the Bazaar

were always a few conservative villagers around—probably recently arrived from Anatolia in search of work—but most locals dressed as in the West, and behaved as Europeans. They did not gather round to inspect a new car, nor did they stared unashamedly at strangers—a village habit which seemed to disconcert many travellers. They ate with proper cutlery and set their hair in fashions copied from imported glossy magazines. Most men did not indulge in the general village habit of flattening the backs of their shoes so as to avoid the bother of tying up the laces, and many actually polished their shoes, and even went to the trouble of pressing their trousers, something which was still unheard of in Anatolia.

Gradually, however, as the weeks of winter passed, the barriers of hospitality erected by the Algans fell down, and their true family life began to emerge—and as it did so, it reminded me strongly of life in Ortahisar. Mr Algan appeared as the undisputed head of the house, with authority equal to that of any male in Ortahisar. He could send the women packing to the kitchen, forbid his wife to visit the cinema, or complain of bad cooking without batting an eye—indeed it seemed like the most natural thing in the world. The authority of the male sex seemed even more obvious in the case of Nezih the son: his mother, worried about his poor exam marks at school, was silenced with a quick slap across the face! And Merih, his little sister, unfortunately at the giggly schoolgirl age, was also often walloped. Moreover, when it suited Şefik *baba*, he would revert to the traditional custom of eating only with the men-folk—his son, sons-in-law, and myself—and the women would merely serve the food.

Mrs Algan, however, had her bright moment on her monthly 'at home' day, when her friends would descend on the house for glasses of tea—and when her husband found it wiser to be elsewhere. Also Merih, the youngest daughter, gradually found it easier to blether with me, and I took up English lessons with her, using the words of current pop songs. She still refused to be seen alone with me in public, however, and always took one of her nieces or nephews along when we went shopping—just for appearance's sake, she explained.

Despite winter's harshness, I was able to visit European Istanbul quite often, particularly during early February. Although I spent most of my time at the Bazaar, I also tried to visit more of the city, now that there were virtually no tourists to distract me. I also spent a lot of time in the various Archaeological Institutes which dotted the Galata and Beyoğlu quarters of the city, and by reference to seemingly little-used volumes in their libraries, I began to learn more of the rock churches at Göreme (though all that emerged was that few writers have ever understood much about the community, except its art, which still provides plenty of argument over 'influences' and 'styles'). Indeed, I felt that my own ideas were probably just as valid.

One of my great pleasures, however, was to go rooting among forgotten back-streets in the city, where I discovered a wealth of history—much more than could be gleaned from visiting Istanbul's obvious tourist sites—for much of the old Byzantine city lay just beneath the surface, if I was prepared to go looking for it. Many of the city's mosques used to be Byzantine churches, and in the Little Aya Sofya mosque I discovered what had once been the Church of Sergius and Bacchus, built by the Emperor Justinian in gratitude to these two saints for having once saved his life. By wandering around the back-streets near the buildings of the Greek Patriarchate, I also discovered the Byzantine church of St Mary Moukhliotissa, built in 1261 and still used by Greeks to this day—the only Byzantine building still fulfilling its original function. Close to the Valens Aqueduct I came across the mosque known as Molla Zeyrek—originally the Church of the Monastery of Christ Pantocrator—in which many of the Comnene and Paleologue emperors were buried. Happily, the original magnificent twelfth-century floor survived, and I was told that archaeologists had even found what they believed were pieces of the original stained glass windows. So by examining only a few mosques I was already discovering for myself something of the old city—history which so often escaped the summer tourists, beset on all sides with advertisements for only the best-known ancient monuments.

A good example, I thought, was the Yerebatan cistern, to

which most tourists were directed, since it lay conveniently between the Bazaar and the Aya Sofya museum. But by making only a short detour, I discovered the Binbirdirek Cistern, built during the reign of Constantine the Great, founder of the Byzantine city. Though a little smaller (224 columns as opposed to Yerebatan's 336), it had greater character, was much older, and was more interesting—yet it seemed to be missed by most people.

Another interesting feature of the old city was the hippodrome. Three columns, standing before the mosque of Sultan Ahmet, were all that survived of this ancient sports arena, but even these columns were of great interest: one, an obelisk, probably a companion to Cleopatra's Needle, was brought to Constantinople in A.D. 390 by Theodosius the Great: the second, a fine bronze pillar of three intertwining snakes, was brought to the city from Delphi by the Emperor Constantine the Great, and the third column, an obelisk of unknown origin, was once decorated with copper sheeting, which was later stolen by soldiers of the Fourth Crusade. Three fine monuments then, and all recalling the fortunes of Byzantium, but all simply glanced at by the summer tourists.

I did not forget to look also for the old Ottoman city. Although the general impression of Istanbul was one of dilapidation and decaying back streets, despite the many modern blocks now being built, a number of interesting Ottoman buildings could still be found, and with the help of Yilmaz from the alabaster shop, we discovered the Çemberlitaş Hammami (Turkish Bath), where during the latter years of the Empire people came for their periodic scrub-downs.

We also looked round the vast palace of Dolmabahçe, and discovered the corridor which led from the sultan's quarters to the Harem—there were nine different doors, with the second and eighth of reinforced steel. But Dolmabahçe was too ornate and Italianesque—only in the beautiful bathrooms of the Harem, built of delicate alabaster in gorgeous shades of ornately-cut stone, survived that old Turkish feeling for light and delicacy, tinkling water and fragrant perfumes. To me the rest of the palace looked like a nineteenth-century monument to Westernisation, hastily constructed in an effort to modernise while the Ottoman Empire gradually crumbled away. Atatürk died in this palace in 1938, and we found the clocks all standing silent, showing the moment of the great man's death. It was as though they mourned not only his passing, but the passing of the best that was traditional as well.

But even ignoring the city's palaces and *hammams*, I did not need to look far for the Ottoman way of life. It survived in the city's many wooden tenements, now being pulled down because of their fire risk, or in the jumble of gloomy caravanserais which crowded down from the Bazaar towards the Galata Bridge. I discovered a couple of little restaurants where I could sample traditional Turkish foods long forgotten by many cafés, and even in winter I was able to find a sherbet water seller, still offering his traditional drink from a spout curving over his shoulder from an urn carried on his back.

So, in spite of Istanbul's efforts to become a modern, European city, there seemed still to be a tremendous amount of history and atmosphere awaiting discovery. I smile now at the naïvety of my first stay in Istanbul, when, because of a veil fluttering on a washing-line, and a few old men sitting sadly by the harbour, I imagined that I had made the vital discovery that the city was not entirely Westernised. I was right in my belief, but I based it on only a fraction of what the city had to offer.

I cannot begin to describe the Bazaar—that 'University of Life' as Mehmet Ali once called it—with all its frantic undercurrents of tension and anxiety, humanity and scum. I used to sit outside the carpet shop watching people passing; there was an old man, bent almost double with age, who used to collect cigarette butts and brush them all carefully into a drain—only the ends of discarded cigarettes. Mehemt Ali himself employed a deaf mute to roll up carpets which had been shown to visitors, and this fellow used to show me whatever he was rolling up, pointing to little facets in the design or weave to indicate some flaw, or some interesting feature. Though we could not communicate, I learned a lot from him. There were also the porters, pathetic creatures who would carry monstrous loads for a few pence—you could always tell a porter at a glance by the way in which he was so bent, even when carrying nothing.

Then there were the prostitutes—one woman, quite attractive, used to visit the shop quite often, but there were also occasions when Mehmet Ali and his friends would suddenly all go off to the city's brothel—a police-supervised, partitioned street near the Galata Bridge, where the girls had a uniformly dull appearance. But even the Bazaar, it was said, could fulfil a man's most unusual demands; villagers from eastern Anatolia were, it seemed, quite prepared to sell their daughters' virginities for handsome sums. Although these girls would later find it very difficult to attract husbands, the cash raised by a day or two in Istanbul would be enough to maintain a family for some weeks. It was a sad business, I felt, but at least I could understand the twinkle in Mehmet Ali's eye when he told me once that the Bazaar could produce anything I wanted, from a sewing needle to an elephant.

Istanbul was undoubtedly an attraction for ladies of negotiable virtue. Girls came from all over Europe to work in the city's many night clubs, but it was also quite possible to find Swedish, German, Italian or French tarts in the city brothel. Illegal establishments also existed and I even heard it claimed that some of Istanbul's most internationally famous hotels were also its most notorious and luxurious brothels. I also heard of 'interesting' Turkish baths, of small-time hotels in the Sultan Ahmet and Sirkici quarters of the old town, and of little men ready to accost people in the streets with a variety of proposals—not entirely surprising perhaps in this centuries-old city of license.

The Bazaar's underworld life was, however, discreet. I only realised its existence because I spent long days in the place. But to the average hurrying visitor, little would have seemed shady; there was a greater possibility of being stopped in the street by unobtrusive characters selling hash—and frequently also in possession of police identification cards. That nothing was actually *seen* to happen in the Bazaar may have been because of the bustling crowds which milled around everywhere, even in winter. But in fact, beneath those crowds, plenty went on. I saw several dozen men disappear into one shop's attic to watch pornographic films recently arrived from Denmark. I saw another little man scurry off with a brand new automatic pistol in his pocket, and yet a third very respectable gentleman produce from his brief-case samples of ammunition for automatic rifles, which he had procured by devious means from Czechoslovakia. And of course there was a widespread black market in foreign currencies. Though the police kept a very sharp eye open for this, the need for dollars, marks and sterling seemed to be ever-present, and no matter how many European countries devalued their currencies, Istanbul seemed always happy to buy cash. Few tourists stayed long in Istanbul without discovering that in the Bazaar they could exchange both cash and travellers' cheques for high, but illegal, rates. Indeed, such dealings seemed almost a way of life.

The Bazaar's main business was, of course, selling. When selling a carpet, there were always certain general rules to follow. Mehmet Ali and his staff sought a civilised approach, preferably over a glass of tea, when trying to make a sale. In general, we also preferred people to express some interest in the wares they were shown, to ask intelligent questions, and by all means to take their time in choosing such an expensive item as a rug. In general, the French gave me the impression of being too agitated, the Americans too brash, and the British far too much out of their depth. The Scandinavians and Swiss created the best impression, but Germans, though perhaps militaristic in approach, were also welcome clients. The occasional Arab popped in, and also a few Latin Americans, but most of our customers were European, and I soon learned to handle each nationality differently. In spite of winter's lack of tourists, however, I still managed a number of sales, much to Mehmet Ali's delight and my own satisfaction. Perhaps my greatest success was the sale of two prayer rugs to my father, who dropped in to see me in March.

The most interesting aspect of the Bazaar, apart from its fascinating swarm of humanity, were the workshops which surrounded it. First I found the adjacent book bazaar, and by prowling around from there, I discovered the street of the copper-beaters. Actually I heard them, and traced the insistent noise of tapping and banging to a back-street, where I found rows of small cubicle-shops, each housing a figure bent over some copper or brass object, carefully tapping it into shape, or patiently carving out some intricate pattern from designs obviously handed down through several generations. Then in another part of the Bazaar I discovered an attic wherein sat a number of youths, all creating 'antique' weapons. In fact, they were taking the best surviving pieces from a pile of disused guns, and then assembling from the least rusted and worm-eaten parts, a number of flint-lock and percussion pistols and muskets. They then inlaid their creations, when necessary, with thin slivers of brass and tin to simulate gold and silver, and in minutes these weapons could be seen on display in the shops of the 'antique' quarter of the building. I also met a suede coat tailor who made measured jackets and coats in a tiny workshop buried deep in the centre of the bazaar. There were joiners, furriers, jewellers—there was seemingly no end to the number of tiny shops, all busily creating more wares to be sold in this fascinating jungle of streets and stalls called the *kapalıçarşi*.

Perhaps the Bazaar's most awe-inspiring sight was its street of gold shops. Sellers of golden jewellery could be found scattered throughout the Bazaar's four thousand shops, but there was one street in particular where almost every shop sold nothing but gold. The very sight of these windows, glittering and sparkling with all that gold on display, was enough to make me feel that this was indeed Aladdin's Cave! This street was simply *fabulous*, though even fabulous hardly does it justice.

Gold shops were a separate concern from the conventional jewellery market because of Turkey's various marriage customs. Although I had not yet attended a village wedding, already I knew that in many parts of Turkey, brides-to-be indicated their betrothal by wearing golden discs—the equivalent of an engagement ring. Gold shops therefore sold thousands of golden discs, particularly for the conservative village element living in Istanbul. I also knew that, once married, a wife expected to receive the occasional token of her husband's continuing affection for her, which he would do by presenting her with occasional golden bangles—so gold shops accordingly sold rows and rows of bangles. And finally, because the Bazaar was in Istanbul, gold shops pandered to the West by selling conventional wedding rings. Thus the overall effect of rows and rows of rings and discs and bangles, all glittering in the light from strategically-placed electric bulbs, was fantastic.

An Istanbul wedding is something that should never be missed if the opportunity arises. I was invited to a wedding which took place in a registry office at Kadiköy, on the Bosphorus's Anatolian shore. The bride-to-be was a relative of the Algan family, so we were all invited.

We drove first to the bride's home, situated some miles outside Istanbul, where we waited for the groom to appear. Soon after all the guests were assembled outside the house, the young man appeared, to loud applause from the crowd, in the wedding car—a limousine specially decked out with ribbons and a large doll dressed as a bride in a Western-style white costume, carefully attached to the front of the bonnet. The groom then disappeared into the bride's house, and the guests fell back to chattering again.

Minutes later the couple appeared, he dressed in a conventional black, formal suit with a lapel flower, she in a beautiful European-style wedding dress with a long train and a discreet veil. People cheered, some of the children threw confetti over the beaming, happy couple as they made for their car . . . and then with a roar and a screeching of brakes and gears, the bridal car surprisingly disappeared! But everyone just laughed as I found myself being hurriedly pushed into another car, and in no time we were off in pursuit of the groom. As we tore along, with the speedometer rising at an alarming rate, the driver explained to me the reason for the rush.

'You see, if I can stop the groom's car, then he must pay me a fine in order to get past! If he can't pay the fine, he won't get to the registry office and he won't get married!' The driver laughed heartily, put his foot down further, and swerved wildly to avoid a stray hen.

'So all these cars are chasing the groom . . . are we the only people who can stop him?'

'Oh no!' shouted the driver above the crashing of his gears. 'Anyone can stop him—you can always tell a bridal car by the doll. But supposing you were a petrol pump attendant and you saw the car approaching . . . there isn't much you could do to stop it, is there!' He was laughing and laughing, all the time drawing slowly closer to the beribboned car ahead. Our Mercedes dodged smartly past a slower Volkswagen, and with the bridal car now in our sights we set off in grim pursuit, with the driver still laughing away to himself.

Istanbul's outskirts flashed past almost in a blur, and I grinned at a policeman standing helplessly by the road with his hand pushed out hopefully towards the groom's car. We flitted past him, still with his hand out, but now looking rather bewildered, and gradually we closed up on the car ahead, which now started to swerve across the road in an effort to prevent us from passing. Suddenly we were screeching along the pavement, but then we had to swerve back on to the road again because of an approaching bridge. . . . And eventually, with much triumphant horn tooting, the groom's car reached the registry office, undefeated and still with its doll attached to the bonnet. Shakily, the young couple disappeared into the office, and were followed by the other guests as they arrived.

Once inside, we looked around for the bride and groom, but they had disappeared, so I took a seat in the main hall, which before long was full with guests taking the opportunity to catch up on forgotten family gossip. Then a hush fell as the couple appeared, and together they sat down at a table where sat the registrar, accompanied by an official witness. The registrar read out the usual marriage vows, everyone at the table signed his book, and soon the couple were man and wife.

The smiling pair then stood by the door as we all filed out, with our congratulations and best wishes for the future. And to each guest was given a tiny beribboned box of sweetmeats from which to nibble on the return journey to the bride's home. One by one the cars left the registry office and motored more leisurely back the way they had all come. Then at a hotel near the bride's home, we took our places round a vast banquet table and received the newly-married couple with toasts.

Dinner was accompanied by a traditional Turkish cabaret, and I recalled the 'wedding salon' wherein I had played the guitar for Volkan. On this occasion there was no jester, but we had our belly and oriental dancers, voluptuous singers, and skilled instrumentalists. By the end of the dinner, several guests also wanted to perform, and to the music of attendant stringed instruments there appeared a succession of rather lubricated gentlemen, performing with varying degrees of ability several ancient Turkish dances. These were followed by many of the younger guests, taking over as their parents tired out. To my surprise Merih, the Algan daughter, turned out to be an oriental dancer of some skill, and the crowd watched with great enthusiasm as she and her father performed several intricate movements. Even the professional dancers applauded as father and daughter left the floor, and as we all returned to Bostanci, Merih and Şefik *baba* were still smiling with triumph.

That wedding, as events proved, marked a turning point in my Turkish stay, for not long after, Selma *anne* began to talk of her daughter's need to get married. I personally felt that this little girl, still a giggly school pupil, was far too young to be getting married, but Mrs Algan explained that in her family the normal age for marriage had always been around thirteen or fourteen: she herself had been married at twelve and had borne children when aged only thirteen and fifteen. Her daughters Ayla and Ayfer had also married at thirteen, though to men considerably older; Ayfer's husband Yalçin had been twenty-six when he married his barely teenage wife.

Selma *anne* explained that among conservative families, marriages were still privately arranged. In general, girls married husbands introduced to them by their parents—this avoided the possibility of either party hearing of some past indiscretion, knowledge of which might influence the eventual decision to marry. Girls especially knew that their chances of marriage would drop considerably should they ever be seen alone in the company of a boy, even more so should they be caught illicitly holding hands. And should anyone find a girl actually *kissing*, then her chances of marriage would become virtually nil, at least in her own neighbourhood—hence Merih's reluctance to be seen alone with me in public.

Anyway, the Algan daughters were normally married off at around thirteen years of age. State law had, since the days of Atatürk, demanded that girls wait until the age of sixteen before marrying, but this had since been amended to allow girls to marry sooner on production of a letter of consent from the parents of both parties. Mrs Algan was now looking for a husband for Merih—someone whose parents would agree to such an early marriage.

The system of family marriages in Istanbul seemed to be as follows. The girls' parents would look around for an agreeable groom, and would select one generally from hearsay or by introduction through a non-involved party. Having found a suitable young man, probably in his twenties, and therefore already earning, they would then invite his family round for tea. This would give the couple an opportunity to meet each other (surrounded by their assembled relatives), and during this meeting impressions would be formed.

The hopeful girl would usually serve the tea, and would try to be as gracious and competent as possible. She would not have seen the young man before, however, and if she did not like him she would never see him again. After tea, the visitors would depart, and both families would ask their young hopefuls what they thought of the other. If either reply was negative, the other family would be informed accordingly, while if the answer was yes, another afternoon-tea session would be arranged. Should the young couple's feelings be unchanged after a second meeting, the two families would organise a betrothal and a party would be held, serving the function of advertising the proposed wedding.

At this stage either party could still have second thoughts and back out, which, though this would cause considerable loss of family face, would still be preferable to an unhappy marriage. Once this rather vague betrothal was converted into a definite engagement, the opportunities for backing out would be vastly reduced, and indeed could provoke family vendettas.

Thus, while marriages were family-arranged affairs, a young couple would have a certain amount of say in their destinies, for a girl could, theoretically, refuse many suitors until she found one to whom she was positively attracted. The drawback seemed to be that word could pass around that so-and-so was difficult to please. So it seemed that, although traditions governed many aspects of wife-hunting, custom had evolved and remoulded itself to suit modern times and pressures.

Then I suddenly found myself becoming unpopular with the local Bostanci youth, and soon I had to leave our pop group. It transpired that they were jealous of my privileged life within the Algan household, wherein lived Merih, whom many local boys wanted eventually to marry (as they now angrily explained to me). Local public opinion was roused against me, and for some weeks I was unable to appear in the streets alone. When I did, I found myself threatened with pistols and wicked-looking knives by gangs of boys, sometimes even supported by the local police, who had already allowed a poster bearing my photograph to be pinned up outside their office, appealing to the public to beat me up and drive me out of town. I was frequently challenged to fights, and then found that my persistent refusals to be drawn into physical violence only made things worse. Once extra hooligans were even imported from Istanbul itself to assist in my expulsion.

The Algan family rode this crisis with tremendous dignity. In addition to the hooligan element, several local adults also began protesting against the acceptance of an infidel bachelor into the everyday confines of a Moslem home, apparently with full freedom and liberty as if he were a member of the family. The Algans resisted all criticism stoutly, and sometimes they met other families to explain the position, but inevitably I was one day approached on the delicate subject of marriage to Merih.

This had already been made easier by my father, who had written from Britain admiring some Algan family photos, and in particular Merih's fast-improving looks . . . she had certainly changed dramatically over the winter! (During the following summer she entered the Miss Turkey competition, and reached the last fifteen girls before the judges discovered that she was only aged thirteen—four years younger than the minimal age for entry!) Anyway, father's praise for Merih was considered significant. . . .

I agreed to the initial betrothal for a number of reasons. I wanted to delay Merih's marriage to anyone for as long as possible, until she reached a suitable mentality and maturity. I also got on well with her, and was supremely happy living with the Algans, whom I rated among my greatest friends; in particular I had been accepted by the Algan men as one of them. Merih would also be an indisputably faithful wife, obedient and hard-working, which to a teenage young man seemed a good idea. And of course I also agreed because I loved Merih, partly infatuation, partly as a great friend.

My father, on his way to South-East Asia, dropped in to Istanbul to visit the Algans and to size up the wedding situation. He seemed to find Merih's femininity very attractive, and left with a favourable impression of them all, having wined, dined, and done his fair share of dancing as a guest of the family. His only proviso was that the Algans should agree to wait at least a year before taking the betrothal any further. My uncle and aunt then arrived on a cruise in early March, and having followed me around the city's main tourist sites for the day, spent the evening with the Algans, where there appeared another awesome spread and another orgy of oriental dancing, during which Merih also won their hearts. So it seemed that the stage was set for a Turco-Scottish wedding.

Then Merih suddenly turned awkward, much to everyone's disappointment, but predictably perhaps, for she did not want to leave her mother, or her street and country. She demanded conditions—I must agree to live in Istanbul and not in Britain and I must agree to become a Moslem. In essence, she was, as I had always believed, simply not yet ready for marriage. And so, as she grew increasingly demanding throughout the spring and summer, the possibility of marriage became more remote.

Perhaps I should explain how my betrothal ended. Merih spent the remainder of my stay in Turkey sometimes anxiously agreeing to the marriage, sometimes bitterly attacking it, so much so that no one, including herself, knew what she really wanted. This uncertainty led to an increasing hostility against everyone involved in the original idea, and for months she was dreadfully insolent to her family, so during my last few days in the city before returning home I decided to live elsewhere, only visiting the Algans occasionally.

I wrote several times to Merih on my return to Britain, but received no replies. Eventually I got an apologetic letter from Selma *anne* and Ayla, Merih's sister, both of whom suggested that because of Merih's refusal to write, I ought to drop the betrothal. They were ashamed of Merih's inexcusable behaviour, they said, and added that there would be no bitterness should I break off the betrothal, as she deserved. Eventually I wrote, and the betrothal was ended.

I returned to Istanbul the following summer, however, and remembering the Turkish custom of not allowing a girl to see a male after a refusal to marry, I rather nervously phoned the Algans. But all went well—I was enthusiastically welcomed, spent an enjoyable day in Bostanci, and renewed my friendship with Merih, who now happily referred to me as her big brother.

Today, all is forgotten and I am once more a welcome guest in the Algan home. Local hooligans have all disappeared—some of them into jail—and neighbours are now all firm friends. Perhaps most important of all, I have learned that in Turkey, too much runs too deep for me ever to be able to understand the various currents of life. Then, I succeeded in discovering an old way of life in Istanbul . . . now I have discovered that I cannot share in that life, but can only hang around its fringe like a moth trying to reach a light, but so rarely succeeding. . . .

March saw a remarkable improvement in the weather, and with this there also occurred the Kurban *bayram* or Festival of the Ram, which passed in an orgy of eating mutton, sharing food with neighbours and the poor, and attending the local mosque. After this, I began to feel that I should leave Istanbul and go back to Ortahisar, where work called. But now I was reluctant to leave the cosy comfort of city life, despite the long journey each day to Mehmet Ali and his carpet shop, and I delayed my departure.

As spring arrived, bringing with it sunshine and greenery, we started eating outside, under a copse of trees near the house. These picnics became another great pleasure for me, and I began to regret the odd day when dull weather forced us indoors again. I also visited the Emirgan Park, situated far up the Bosphorus beyond the fabulous ruins of Rumeli Hisar, and from where tulip bulbs were first taken to Holland. Though it was too early to enjoy the sight of Istanbul's famous tulip gardens, I was assured that in season, the city could offer no greater pleasure.

In March I was also accorded one of the greatest possible Islamic compliments when I was invited to accompany Selma *anne*'s son-in-law Emin, who was a doctor, to a circumcision ceremony. These ceremonies, performed on young boys of about seven or eight years old, and the equivalent of Christian baptism, were very private affairs I was told, and so when I was taken into the house of an ultra-conservative village family recently arrived from the interior, I was indeed aware of the honour which I was being accorded. I was, after all, an infidel.

We arrived to find the family men-folk already there, and two little boys already waiting with a mixture of pride and fear in their eyes. As Emin arranged his instruments, a table was brought and the boys were placed on top. Then as the operation began, all the men crowded round and began to sing a soulful melody, reminding the boys to be brave and to be proud of becoming fully-fledged Moslems. There was no anaesthetic, but as the knife cuts appeared, the wounds were healed with a putty substance, and then dressed in spotless white bandages. The men's singing reached a climax, and then Emin rolled down his sleeves with satisfaction, and the lads managed a weak smile.

But this was not the end, for the little heroes were now taken into the living room where the women had been waiting, and there they were dressed in white shirts decorated with red sashes, and then tucked up in a special bed by one wall. And then a celebratory party began, with sas musicians appearing from nowhere, bottles of raki being produced from inside pockets, and *lokum* being passed round the growing numbers of guests. Emin was paid a handsome fee, in spite of the poverty of the family concerned, but he returned most of it as a present to the little boys who now surveyed the party from their bed. A belly dancer appeared, and Nezih also did a wonderful turn as a magician—he had a real talent, in the David Nixon image, and in fact accompanied Emin on many of his operations, often to distract the patients with his wizardry while the operations were being performed. And so the circumcision celebrations went on far into the night.

But eventually, perhaps reluctantly, I left for Ortahisar. The weather on the plateau was now milder, so with much handshaking and kissing of hands I boarded a bus and set off for the village. The journey was uneventful and I arrived as night fell. The first thing that I noticed was that the minaret had disappeared.

Two little girls in a main street in Ortahisar

Part of the Independence Day school parade in Ortahisar

Sinassos, a modern Greek painting in the Ayos Vasilios Church

9 *Spring in Ortahisar*

Ortahisar's winter had been murderous, said Tahir. Some winds had been so ferocious that the recently-built minaret had been blown over, and we went to survey the sorry stump that remained. But now, as we wandered through the village, I noticed flowers growing in the shadow of gullies, and little trickles of water flowing where before all had been dust and baked earth. Ortahisar was enjoying a few weeks of precious greenery.

Tahir's mother had completed only one carpet during my absence, and already it had been sold to a visiting merchant. Some neighbours had spent the winter weaving mats, however, and I was at least able to inspect their handiwork. The mats were roughly woven, obviously hard wearing, and were probably designed for domestic use. I could easily imagine them covering rough uncarpeted village floors, although their attractive stripes and bright colours might also make them of interest to tourists, I thought, remembering my need to decorate the inn.

Tourism picked up remarkably quickly in the village, and I had to get down to preparing the inn almost immediately. Most early tourists seemed to belong to bus parties, doing standard trips from Istanbul round various well-known coastal resorts, but now including Göreme in their latest itineraries. In many ways bus parties were, perhaps justifiably, least welcome in Ortahisar. One company, for example, used to send a weekly busload of tourists into Ortahisar as part of a whistle-stop tour round Cappadocia. This bus would park outside the inn, below the balcony of Mustafa's tea-house, and a selection of sun-blotched Europeans would then emerge, stand around the bus door, and from there photograph anything visible—usually the 'castle' rearing skywards at the other end of the main street. Someone would run after the first veiled woman to pass, and others would follow—causing only irritation among the villagers seated on Mustafa's balcony, Sometimes, one intrepid soul would venture down the main street towards the 'castle', where he would discover Faik's antique shop. So everyone would follow to inspect Roman tear-glasses, horse brasses, Byzantine coins and the like—but inevitably no one would buy, despite my offer to translate. Then the courier would give a shout, sixty tourists would scuttle back to the security of their bus, and in ten minutes Ortahisar would have survived another experience.

Ortahisar had actually much more to offer the interested traveller—though most people imagined the towering castle, with its magnificent view, to be the only attraction. Sadly, few individuals recognised Ortahisar's wonderful situation as a centre from which to begin explorations of Göreme, and still fewer realised that within Ortahisar itself lay several sites just as interesting as those buried among the needles of the Fairy Chimneys.

There was, for example, the Cambasli Church, a small chapel buried underneath the castle's pinnacle, and which I rated among the best in the Göreme region. There were the nearby church communities of Tavşanli, Kepez, and Pancarlik, offering points of varying architectural interest, ranging from one unusual shade of blue paint, to relatively rare wall mouldings and altar steps. But like the Cambasli Church, these chapels were rarely visited. Then there was also a series of columned rock chambers thought once to have been Göreme's 'hospital'—so much interesting history, but all missed by the whistle-stop tourist.

One building which had become neglected with the passing of the years was the village library. Travellers used *always* to visit this remarkable place, and many left volumes as a contribution to the shelves. Everyone used at least to sign the visitors' book and from its long list of signatures I could tell for how long Göreme had been known to travellers—since the early 1950's, it seemed.

The library used also to be the main centre of village education, taking over from the mosque towards the end of the last century, and it still housed volumes of tremendous antiquity, plus many books written in French, German, English and Italian, and in particular, translations of the great European classics—I once found Tahir reading *Crime and Punishment* in Turkish, for example. The building now also served as an important centre of agricultural learning, and the librarian collected farming journals and magazines for the use of the villagers. So in many ways the library was still a centre of learning, for it provided literature and reference works quite out of proportion to its rural surroundings. This was often a surprising discovery for visitors and my only regret was that so few people, in this age of hurried itineraries, could be bothered to visit this little library.

The library was also the base for a local village lending service, rather like a mobile bookshelf, for books were taken round neighbouring hamlets by donkey. Ortahisar was justly proud of its donkey service, and the expansion of education which had resulted, and photographs of the inauguration ceremony hung in the library.

Lucky visitors sometimes also arrived during one of Ortahisar's many festivals or parades, held primarily on the anniversary of Atatürk's death, on Youth Day, Independence Day, and so on.

On these occasions, the village children, dressed in gay traditional costumes, often family heirlooms, would march from their primary school to the market square in front of the municipal offices, where they would then listen to speeches from the village mayor. On Independence Day they would also repeat slogans into a microphone, rather like children in China, but much to the appreciation of admiring parents, and indeed, with dancing to follow, the scene was usually a very colourful one.

Even the little village school was of interest, for how many visitors, I wondered, knew about Turkey's education system? So I made it my job to introduce tourists to the school, if they so wished.

At that time, Ortahisar had only a Lower School, although I was told that a Middle School was to be built soon. Pupils graduating from Ortahisar went to a Middle School in Ürgüp, from where the cleverest continued to the High School in Nevşehir. Attendance at the Lower School was compulsory, but free. Middle and High School education cost fees, however, and for this reason alone, many of Ortahisar's children never received more than an elementary education.

The village school was opened in 1928, and replaced an old Arabic class which had until then been held in the library. At that time, only Turkish, writing, and the Koran were taught: before 1890, the only education available in Ortahisar took the form of Koran readings in the mosque. But with the appearance of Kemal Atatürk at the head of Turkish government, educational reforms were made, and elementary schools appeared in almost every village. After 1928, new timetables were also created, and now I found the school teaching Maths, Turkish, History, Geography, Biology, Music, Drawing, and Home Economy—quite a handful for children aged only from seven to twelve years.

The school had roughly four hundred pupils, divided into five years, with classes averaging around thirty to forty pupils. Because of a teacher shortage, a shift scheme operated, and pupils attended only from 9 a.m. to 12.30 or from 1 p.m. to 4.15. The teachers, however, worked from 8.30 a.m. to 4.15 p.m. five days a week, plus a half day on Saturday, when shorter shifts were run.

I was told that about twenty per cent of pupils attending the Lower School would carry on to the Middle School at Ürgüp, where they would join pupils from other surrounding Lower Schools. From there about ten pupils, not all from Ortahisar, would graduate each year to the High School at Nevşehir, though a few more would opt for teacher training schools instead, where they would qualify as teachers for Lower Schools. Most pupils reaching High School would continue to some kind of university—but clearly, not many children from Ortahisar would ever reach Higher Education.

Ortahisar's school teachers were all graduates from a teacher training institute, and about half were women. The headmaster *may* have been to High School, but he had not attended a university—no university graduate would settle for the underpaid job as head of a Lower School. Teachers to whom I spoke in Ortahisar were paid from 450 Turkish Lira (£18) per month starting salary, to 700 T.L. (£28) per month after twelve years' service. Someone said that the Teachers' Union wanted a rise of around 50 T.L. per month for every three years of service, but because of the Union's very weak position this seemed an unlikely eventuality.

At present insufficient teachers lived in the village, so a mini-bus brought additional staff from Ürgüp each morning. Most of these Ürgüp teachers were women, which caused some discontent in the village, for Ürgüp's female teachers dressed in skirts as part of the general effort being made to Europeanise Turkey, and their new fashions were frowned upon by the village women. Village women actually stoned the mini-bus once, but Ürgüp's teachers were for the most part tolerated, if only because there was no one else to teach the children.

Tourists began to trickle in to the village as spring progressed, and the inn's business gradually began to improve. Carpets sold well, and postcards also made some money. Surprisingly, however, some visitors laughed at, even scorned, our humble efforts to improve the inn's efficiency and usefulness, and sometimes I wondered if my efforts were being wasted.

On one notable occasion we received a pile of paperback books, copies of a simple guide to the Göreme region written in German and Turkish. The innkeeper, however, kept these in his room, and for weeks we sold nothing, until I realised this. I suggested they should be displayed, but the innkeeper replied that since he could not be present all day, someone might steal a copy. Nevertheless, I persuaded him to put the books on display, so that they would catch the attention of tourists—and within the week a copy was removed. . . . How was I to introduce improvements when I could get no support from my own people?

On another occasion we were honoured with the arrival of M. and Mme. Thierry, authors of a distinguished volume on the rock churches of Western Cappadocia. The village was proud to receive the Thierrys, and almost everyone who could walk inspected their classy expedition Land-Rover. I, meanwhile, had posted a notice written in English, German, Dutch, Turkish and French, advertising the availability of the paperback guide-book. Before leaving, Mme Thierry scrawled *nombreuse erreurs* under the French paragraph, and then signed it—an unnecessary comment, I felt, particularly since the poster could have been written by some enterprising villager, and also since the meaning was still perfectly obvious.

With the arrival of more tourists, guiding business also began to improve, and during the ensuing weeks I made a number of trips into surrounding Cappadocia, leading a variety of visitors, some very keen and observant, a few rather worried by being in unfamiliar country. Kurt and Hermann for example were two middle-aged Germans from somewhere near Munich, who arrived, predictably enough, in a Volkswagen. Their hobby was collecting bits of ruins, which they were building into a garden wall at home. They had already acquired little pieces of Jericho, Nineveh, Jerusalem, Ur, and so on, and were now heading for Troy, Ephesus, and other popular sites on the Aegean coast. While in Ortahisar, they asked me to show them around Cappadocia.

First we visited the 'underground cities' at Kaymakli and Derinkuyu. On emerging from the tunnels, Kurt said:

'Ve haff seen the same in Kieff. Ven ve voss in Kieff, ve ver visiting the underground monasteries, vere ve ver kindly received by the monks. . . . Vot a fascinating place!'

'Oh yes? I'm afraid I've not yet visited the underground monasteries at Kiev. When were you there?'

Kurt looked somewhat sheepish. 'Vell, you see, it voss mit ze Panzers in 1941. . . .'

Rather embarrassed, therefore, we drove on to Niğde, a town whose history we found hard to decipher. It boasted an archaeological museum which included the mummified corpse of a Christian woman, found in a sixth-century chapel at Peristrema (another collection of monasteries), and we also found a ruined caravanserai and some beautiful Seljuk and Ottoman tombs and mosques. But as a place of some historical importance, there was surprisingly little left to see. However, the town was a good centre for excursions to other local Hittite and Byzantine sites, and so under my guidance we set off for the underground monastery of Eski Gümüș.

Eski Gümüș was, for me, a site of considerable interest. Excavated and restored by the British Institute of Archaeology at

Ankara, it consisted of a rock-cut monastery built around a central courtyard, itself completely hacked out of the local tufa rock. The community survived, it is believed, from roughly 1050–1150, when it was overrun by the Seljuks, but during that brief century, its monks created some of Cappadocia's most remarkable paintings. One fresco, of the Virgin and Child, I ranked among the finest I had seen anywhere in the province.

The monastery's art was, for me, its main attraction. The frescoes, lacking Egyptian or Syrian influence, were, in fact, now considered to be major examples of provincial Byzantine Renaissance work, thus paralleling the Apple and Dark Churches at Göreme (though some scenes did resemble certain frescoes at Ochrid in Yugoslavia, in particular one famous painting of the 'Doctors of the Church'). And as we surveyed this row of solemn ecclesiastics, Kurt nodded knowingly—perhaps he already had a piece of Ochrid for his garden wall!

The most interesting chamber at Eski Gümüş was one we found by accident, leading off from an upstairs corridor. Some solitary monk had obviously been doodling with his brushes here—for all along one wall were scenes from Aesop's fables. We managed to pick out 'The man bitten by the ungrateful snake', 'The wolf mocked by the lamb', and 'The eagle pierced by an arrow'. How fascinating were those sketches, even though Aesop's morals were hardly those of an eleventh-century monastery!

Unfortunately, Kurt and Hermann soon found the rock paintings all too similar so we moved on. Eventually we got lost in the middle of the night, and unexpectedly found ourselves returning to Ortahisar along a rocky river-bed, already awash with floods from recently-melted snows. I felt secretly pleased at this revenge against my employers for not having visited more churches!

Franco, on the other hand, was a genial Swiss Italian who was happy to see anything—provided we walked there. His unfortunate passion was for walking, as in his mountains at home, and since no amount of persuasion would deter Franco from striding off into the blistering heat of Göreme's rocks, I jogged along behind. We seemed to whizz round Göreme in record time, and soon I was panting behind him on the long trail to Avanos, passing those now familiar needles and spires to the right, meanwhile hoping that Franco wouldn't suddenly swerve off to visit Çavuşin or Zilve. Thankfully he didn't, and we soon reached Avanos where I speedily wheeled my employer into my customary restaurant, and thankfully sat down in its shade. While Franco investigated the kitchen, I fell into conversation with the café's owner—it was our first meeting in the New Year.

'Well, where are you off to this time?' he inquired, pouring out the usual wine.

'Oh, the pottery and the onyx-works I suppose. . . . Anything else would kill me, the rate he walks at!'

'Oh . . . why don't you visit the tunnels?' he said, wiping his brow with a greasy hand. 'No one seems to go there.'

'Tunnels?'

'Yes . . . you know . . . they have tunnels and things at Özkönak. . . .'

So as soon as lunch was over, off we went in a dolmuş to the village of Özkönak, my spine tingling with the excitement of a possible New Discovery, Franco mumbling away in Italian about why weren't we walking there. Eventually we reached the village, where a visit to the tea-house produced a number of locals willing to guide us to the tunnels. So off we went, across fields and down valleys, following these men until, with a flourish of the hand, they indicated the Underground City of Özkönak.

I would not claim to be the first Britisher ever to visit the site, but our guides said that, so far as *they* could recall, no other foreigners had previously investigated the tunnels. But with no equipment, not even matches, we could undertake little exploration of the passages, even though we had clearly stumbled upon a city, possibly as big as Kaymakli or Derinkuyu, all because of a chance remark in a restaurant. . . .

When I returned, better equipped, to explore the tunnels a year later, I found a guide already installed, and electric lighting fitted down many of the broader passages. I had missed my golden opportunity. . . .

It was Tahir who suggested that we should visit the local village of Sinassos, a once-Greek community wherein I might study modern Orthodox art and architecture, for the village had been Christian until 1924. Eventually we set off in a borrowed jeep, in the company of Ali, a customs officer spending his holiday leave in Ortahisar.

We spent some time wandering around modern Greek churches, admiring the freshness of their paintings, regretting the extensive damage caused by local vandals, examining the village's three monasteries, and discovering a *tuvalet* obviously once used by local monks—about the only advance made in local architecture since about the tenth century, so far as I could see! Then we visited the church of Constantine and Helene, standing sadly in the village market-place: the owner told us that he wanted to turn the building into a museum, but when I returned a year later, nothing had changed. Inscribed slabs still lay around collecting dust, carvings and statues still lay discarded in corners, paint still peeled off the church's columns and ceiling.

Then, while we were on our way to Ayos Vasilios, easily the finest church in Sinassos, Ali suddenly stooped to pluck some weeds.

'Marijuana,' he said blandly. 'I once caught a fellow bringing this stuff over the frontier from Persia—he got nine years, I'm told. Seems silly when we grow it in Turkey. . . .'

Then we drove back to Ürgüp, where we were to dine with, of all people, Tahir's Middle School teacher.

We entered a secluded courtyard and we were met by the teacher (a girl in her twenties), her young sister, and their mother. Following Turkish manners, we all removed our shoes and put on the slippers provided. Then our charming female hostesses sat us down on cushioned divans where we drank tea and nibbled at a variety of nuts, and chattered pleasantly. How agreeable it was to sink back into deep carpeting, with nuts lying handy on one side, a glass of tea on the other, and three vivacious, and for once unveiled, ladies continually inquiring after my comfort! A rather pleasant sample of Oriental luxury, I thought.

It was only after some moments that I noticed everyone had

frozen like pillars of salt . . . I had been talking with Tahir's teacher about her job, when the sudden lull in conversation made us look up. Everyone was sitting with their eyes wide open, their mouths open, unable to speak for some terrible fear.

'Scorpion!' squeaked the mother, her eyes fixed on the floor.

My first instinct was to run, but some sense shouted at me that this would be foolish, for the insect might be anywhere. So gingerly I looked around for the scorpion . . . and found it literally *under* the half-raised bare foot of Tahir's teacher, crouching sinisterly, its fearful tail curled up towards the biggest toe ready to strike at any sudden movement.

'Slowly . . .' I said. 'Raise your foot very slowly . . .'

The foot inched upwards, the vile insect lay momentarily exposed, and in a flash Ali crushed it with a blow from his slipper.

'I . . . I saw it moving right across the floor, until it stopped under my daughter's foot . . .' whispered the mother, still half-petrified with fear.

'Oh you shouldn't worry. It was a red one. I only notice the black ones,' said Ali.

One unforgettable event in Ortahisar was the arrival of Ralph and Stu, for their white-painted Land-Rover had a large sign along one side which read, *Afghanistan here we come!* While this was interesting, the fact that Stu then appeared with a white Persian cat in tow *on a lead* simply put the village into hysterics of laughter, and made my subsequent guiding arrangement rather embarrassing. Stu, however, would not be parted from her precious cat, so in the end we set off with the animal perched precariously in the rear, lost among vast piles of luggage.

We decided to visit Peristrema—perhaps my best guiding coup, for this was a site which could only be reached by Land-Rover, and Ralph's was the first available four-wheel drive, long-base, high-and-low-ratio geared vehicle to appear in Ortahisar. So off we set, first to Nevşehir, then south towards Kaymakli and Derinkuyu, where we paused to visit the tunnels and churches, and then westwards into those incredibly bleak Melendiz Hills. Villages seemed lost in this hilly country of scrub and stony, crudely-cultivated fields; indeed the occasional hamlet clustered round its modern schoolhouse appeared in welcome contrast to the dismally bleak surroundings.

We discovered that Peristrema, now the tiny village of Bellisirma, had once been one of several formerly-Christian communities buried away in the seclusion of the Melendiz Hills—once the sanctuary of so many hermits during the era of Roman persecutions. I was surprised that the rock churches had taken their name from this small village, for they actually lay straggled along the bottom of a gorge, through which flowed the River Melendiz—one of the few permanently-flowing rivers in the area. Peristrema lay above this gorge, while the churches nestled in several nooks and bends of the gorge itself, along its entire six or seven mile length, and not just around the village. Indeed, we had to drive past Peristrema and enter the gorge at the village of Selima, before we could begin to scramble through bushes and over many fallen boulders towards the first of the churches.

To the layman, the chapels which we visited seemed remarkably similar to the underground churches at Göreme and elsewhere. But armed with the Thierrys' remarkable book* on the area, we discovered that in fact there were many differences. Some painted churches dated from as early as the fifth and sixth centuries, for example, and were therefore older than anything at Göreme. Later churches had also been strangely receptive to unusual influences prevalent at the time of their decoration: hence sixth-century chapels featured distinctly Arabic non-figurative ornamentation, some later structures displayed traces of Roman and post-Sassanid influences, and the most recently-created churches even boasted occasional Seljuk patronage, evident by a few illustrations of local Moslem rulers and dignitaries—all non-Christian sources of inspiration.

The collection of chapels at Peristrema seemed also to be unique in the subject matter of the frescoes. One church boasted a scene of the Twenty-Four Elders, Syrian in origin and otherwise totally unknown in Cappadocia. In another case, a painting of

* Thierry, N. and M.: *Nouvelles Églises Rupèstres de Cappadoce: Région du Hasan Daği*. Paris, 1963.

the Devil whispering into Judas' ear was also unique in Cappadocia, while there were also very rare examples of the Denial of Peter, the Magi (wearing trousers), the Virgin at the Well, and the Washing of Jesus' Feet. Another church also boasted a fresco in which the inscriptions were in Babylonian—apparently unique in Byzantine iconography. And finally, one more church, built somewhere between 1283–95, two centuries after the arrival of the Seljuks, enjoyed the distinction of being the most recent rock church in the province, and was to be regarded as a major example of the tolerance which the Islamic Turks had for foreign religious sects caught up in the expansion of the Seljuk empire. The Peristrema collection, then, was unique in many different ways.

The trouble was that no one seemed to be visiting this remarkable gorge—it remained one of the least known sites in Turkey. We stumbled upon a small expedition from Japan—students of art working under their professor—who had been living among the churches for three months: we were the first non-Turks to meet them. And the fellow who led us around the valley added that in all his time as a guide, he had met only the Thierrys (working for several years on their book), and a few professors from Turkish universities. I felt quite pleased to have been one of such a small and select band of visitors, and I think that Ralph and Stu shared that pleasure—but what a shame it is that so much of Turkey remains unknown to tourists simply because it lies just off the beaten track.

Liz, on the other hand, was a friend from Scotland who on my advice dropped into the village while holidaying in Turkey. At first no one seemed to notice her much, so easily did she blend into the surroundings. We went together to a wedding where she danced very self-consciously among the womenfolk, while hordes of men watched from surrounding rooftops. We went to various parties laid on in her honour and again she fitted in quietly, picking up words of greeting and sampling several unusual dishes, but still remaining unobtrusive. In short, Liz ranked among Ortahisar's less noteworthy visitors, causing little offence and making some friends. So when I asked Kazim the horse-dealer for the loan of a horse for Liz, he merely smiled broadly, gladly accepted a *raki* as part of the deal, and promised to provide his finest animal later in the day.

Liz was called to see the horse in mid-afternoon, and together we followed Kazim through numerous back streets to a small, insignificant farmyard where the horse was now being kept. Neither of us quite expected the magnificent animal which was brought before us, however, for a splendid chestnut stallion, with dignified eyes and a tremendous sense of poise appeared, crossed the courtyard haughtily and stood contemplating us with a mixture of pride and softness in its deep eyes. Then with a slow look round at the few spectators, it nuzzled into Kazim's expert palm, to feel communion with its friend. This was a steed to rival any horse ever raised on the Cappadocian plains!

We followed Kazim and the horse into the street outside. Then with a friendly smile he offered the stallion to Liz, who took the simple reins, vaulted into the saddle and set off towards the car-park. Men watched with amazement from the tea-house balcony as she appeared below them, riding confidently on this wonderful stallion. Elbows nudged, faces appeared, and soon a crowd began to gather in the streets as the word flashed round that a *woman* was out riding a horse—a sight that was revolutionary, and not altogether very pleasing.

Before long great numbers of people, anxious to watch Liz's riding, were hurrying towards the car-park. At first she did not seem to notice them, and for some time executed a number of controlled movements, quite unaware of the crowd's stupefaction—to ride the horse was bad enough, but to have complete control over the animal was to put Ortahisar's men to shame . . . and many of them did not like it. Several villagers started shouting and demanding that they too be allowed to show off, but Liz didn't understand them, and meanwhile rode off for a few minutes' gallop, leaving a bewildered and vaguely angered crowd behind. When she returned, it was to find a queue of villagers all demanding a ride on the horse—obviously to put her back into her woman's place.

Several men had a go. Some of them were not so good, a few

were obviously better than Liz. But as more and more people had a turn, a murmur of admiration began to creep round the assembled village gathered to watch this battle of the sexes. Then one little lad appeared with a new horse—a frisky young Arab colt with a wild look in its eye, as if to say that it for one would never be tamed by an upstart female. And just to make the point, it gave a buck and a vicious back-heel as it was presented to Liz.

'Try that one for size!' someone shouted.

'Now we'll separate the *real* riders from the amateurs!'

'You won't last seconds on this one!' jeered someone else.

Fortunately Liz did not understand these unkind comments. She swung up on to the saddle, felt the reins for a moment, and then with a flicker of the heels was off on a headlong gallop into the distance, leaving a speechless crowd around Kazim. Evening was now falling, however, and just as Liz turned a bend on the road, a car swung round towards her, its headlamps glaring in the fast-descending gloom of dusk. The colt reared violently, shying away from the piercing headlamps; Liz fought for control, but then in seconds had disappeared round the bend. With satisfied smiles a number of men went off to pick up the corpse—but before they had walked twenty paces, Liz reappeared, cantering back towards the village with supreme unconcern. Handing the horse back to Kazim with sincere thanks, she walked off towards the inn, leaving a crowd of flabbergasted villagers simply watching her go.

I returned one day from a guiding trip to find a bus parked outside the inn, and on entering the hotel, was amazed to find a full-scale pop dance going on in the reception lobby! Bewildered villagers stood around, quite lost for words as throngs of visitors danced to a portable record-player, clearly enjoying themselves and quite oblivious of the unprecedented scenes which they were creating. I supposed that Ortahisar had never seen a dance like this, but what made it more painful to onlookers was that these people were Turks.

'They're from Ankara!' yelled the innkeeper over the din of pop music.

'Ah . . .' said Tahir knowingly, as if that explained everything.

Later I got to know these people at dinner and soon was hired as their guide for the following day. In particular, I made friends with Ömer and Kazim, two students of political science, and through them discovered that this bus trip was one organised by the Inspectorate of Taxes and Budget, in whose office they were presently being employed on a practical course.

The dancing resumed after the meal, with occasional songs accompanied by my guitar to give people a breather. Meanwhile Tahir sat watching, his eyes wide with amazement—the sight of so many Turkish girls in fashionable mini-skirts was too much for him, I think.

'Can I dance too?' he asked eventually.

'Sure . . . I didn't know you could dance modern rhythms!'

'Oh yes . . .' he said proudly. 'I know the tango . . .!'

The following day we set off for Göreme, and from there I went on to Ankara, to be Ömer's guest for a couple of days. The trip round the churches was not successful for some students resented being told their own history by a foreigner, but as far as I was concerned, it was the greatest move of my life—the Avanos restaurant-keeper's face, as forty people trooped in to his tables, was a sight never to be forgotten!

Then we travelled through the night to Ankara and spent the early morning sleeping in Ömer's house before setting out to see some of the sights. I visited the British Institute of Archaeology, the fabulous Hittite Museum, the Citadel, and assorted ruins, but in general I found the city rather disappointing. Before the Greek War, Ankara had been a small market town with a population of around thirty thousand people, but now it had become a vast city of almost a million inhabitants, and the sudden change, I fear, had not been entirely successful. Ankara was now a city of beautifully spaced boulevards, tree-lined avenues, and modern office and apartment blocks—but lurking behind this strikingly attractive façade lay a whole city of slums and peasantry, which I found saddening. In spite of Ömer and Kazim's spontaneous entertainment, Ankara was not a particularly memorable interlude.

My one high spot was a visit to a night club where I saw Erol Büyükburç at work—no one compared in Turkey with this tremendously popular singer—even Tom Jones had to settle for second place.

Ortahisar experienced some pretty odd events during the summer but nothing could have rivalled the sight of a clapped-out old car which was the proud possession of Claude and Françoise. These two rather gentle French hippies arrived in a vast ponderous black sedan which, as it progressed, did so with exceedingly loud bangs and vile curses from the motor. But it was the proud possessor of one distinctive feature, for painted on to the bonnet was an enormous pink elephant! Villagers stood lost for words as this strange vehicle came spluttering to a halt outside the inn—the pink elephant was ridiculous enough, but Claude with his long hair and flowery trousers was too much, and a large crowd of people followed the motley pair wherever they went. Having learned my lesson from Stu and Ralph, I avoided guiding for these two—people might have thought that I *condoned* such eccentric behaviour. I had long learned that when in Ortahisar, do as the locals do.

Nevertheless, it happened that a village wedding began just as this couple arrived, so out of common hospitality, they were invited along to watch the proceedings. Customs were, of course, quite different from Istanbul: processions came and went led by the village band; the celebrations lasted for four days instead of one, with dancing most of the time; the groom had acquired his bride—not over a glass of tea as in Istanbul—but by paying several golden discs for her hand (I recalled the gold-shops at the Kapalıçarşi); and above all, men and women did not celebrate together, but in separate homes (save that the village men could watch the women dancing from surrounding roof-tops—the only time when young girls would remove their veils in public). The most interesting moment came on the last day however: the wailing of clarinets brought me out into the street, where I watched a procession of donkeys being led through the village to the house of the groom—this was the ceremonial display of

Enjoying a *halay*, or traditional men's dance, at an Ortahisar wedding

Kazim the horse dealer, with the horse which Liz rode

Tahir's mother, Mrs Köse, posing in her courtyard

Kemal, a typical Ortahisar farmer

wedding gifts, so I joined the throng which was following, and eventually we reached a small courtyard. Here the men retired once more to the roof-tops, and the women danced in turn below to the tinkle of a tambourine. Eventually, a wizened old hag appeared, leading in the donkeys laden with wedding gifts. Once these had been displayed the old woman examined each present in turn, making scathing comments as she did so. The place was in fits of laughter for no one, it seemed, could do the right thing: those who had given a handsome gift were status-seekers, those who had not were mean and miserly—no one could win except the old woman! And the assembled village enjoyed every moment of the fun.

Suddenly her eye fell on two characters hovering around the courtyard gate. She made a remarkably fast move, and reappeared triumphantly holding Claude, resplendent in a pair of velvet trousers, with poor Françoise tagging along anxiously after her husband. The old hag had a devilish look in her eye as she made Claude stand in the middle of all those women, and for some time loud laughter echoed from the roof-tops.

'Which kind person sent along this lovely belly-dancer then?' she cried out, amidst great laughter and clapping from the assembled guests.

'Dance! Dance for us!' they shouted, as Claude stood sheepishly in the middle of the courtyard. Tambourines rattled and someone played a clarinet. For a moment I think Claude seriously considered the challenge, but suddenly he turned and ran out with his wife Françoise in pursuit, and the place erupted into guffaws and giggles. The wedding was voted easily the best social event of the year, and perhaps still ranks as one of the funniest episodes in Ortahisar's recent history. The next day, the pink elephant beat an ignominious retreat into the distance, never to be seen in Ortahisar again.

10 *Summer and Farewell*

By late June the heat had become intense, the flies were driving me mad, and tourists had begun to appear in greater numbers—partly, I liked to think, because of my efforts to advertise Ortahisar, but perhaps also because the hotel now looked a bit cleaner. The innkeeper was a stubborn man who would not improve anything without much grumbling, and I had constantly to be nagging him to change the sheets and sweep the floors. On one occasion I went to Istanbul for a week to spend my birthday with the Algans and returned to find the inn now being used as a brothel! The next day, however, the spectators on Mustafa's tea-house balcony witnessed the sullen departure of a flabby-faced middle-aged Turkish woman and a rotund German fraulein, and a murmur of approval passed round the men-folk. Somehow, corruption and flaunted sex had no place in sleepy Ortahisar, where everyone knew exactly where the line between the pleasures of a belly dancer's art stopped and the cheapness of a whore began.

As summer arrived, the fruits of my winter language lessons also began to appear. I spent many an entertaining hour on the tea-house balcony watching small boys running after tourists, calling 'Please mister, you want to go to Göreme? Plenty rock churches and paintings! Very cheap!' Fortunately, most visitors were either good-natured or simply glad to find someone who could direct them through Göreme's extraordinary jungle of rock, and in the end, most of my pupils did modestly well and earned a little hard-won cash. I only felt sorry that none of these tourists would ever realise the long hours spent by their guides, swotting over grammar books and lists of verbs. One little chap called Ali had broken his leg, however, and used to sit sadly watching potential custom going to his rivals. But then he hit upon an idea, and for the rest of the summer he made a small fortune as a shoe-shine boy for tired tourists returning from a day's tramping round dusty Göreme!

Although I still did a little guiding myself, I was happy to leave most of the opportunities to my protégés—not just because I wanted to leave Ortahisar with its own guides after my departure, but simply because the summer was growing daily hotter. The snowcap on distant Mount Erciyas was shrinking to a tiny blob of white on the very summit, the few patches of greenery in the village were, one by one, shrivelling up into brownness, and I was beginning to discover an inability to sustain effort in the hot sunshine of the Turkish plateau—or perhaps I was just lazy. Instead, I liked to wander about at my leisure, writing letters for people, handing out the occasional tube of ointment for festering eyes, or more often than not, helping Tahir and his family in their struggle to grow crops in the powdery, rocky earth of their fields.

As I watched Tahir tending his apple trees, or carrying water from the nearest donkey trough several hundred yards away, I kept thinking of my very first day in Ortahisar, when I had been amazed by the variety and size of the vegetables displayed in the early morning light of Nevşehir's market. I had seen the same sight many times since, but somehow that first impression lingered, and now, as I watched Tahir's back-breaking efforts in the fields, with that blistering sun overhead, my amazement grew. I knew in my heart that had I been faced with such overwhelming odds in my struggle for a living, I would probably have thrown it all up and gone off to Ankara or Istanbul to try again. But Tahir, and every villager like him, was prepared to face the odds every day in his life. It occurred to me that, in a sense, here was a hidden link with the past, for although the monks of Göreme, and even the last of their ancestors, were now gone from Cappadocia, the present generation of farmers were facing the same hardships, under the same sun, facing the same problems of irrigation and fertilisation. It was yet another of those intangible strands which I could see linking the past to the present—another realisation which so enriched and added to the enjoyment of life in Ortahisar.

The admission to myself that I could not face the hardships which Tahir took for granted had a humbling effect on me—indeed there were many ways in which Ortahisar, though it did not know it, made me thankful for my own comfortable life. Not only was I spared that endless struggle against nature, or the grinding toil of underdeveloped agriculture, but I also did not have to watch tourists trampling over my hard-won wheat or constantly sampling my few grapes. Nor did I have the dilemma facing every villager, beset on the one hand with toilsome traditional life, with its quality and values and timeless crafts, and on the other hand, with prosperous modern tourism, pre-packed commercialism, labour-saving devices, easy money, and the destruction of values. I was glad to have been spared such difficulties.

One day Tahir decided to sell his crop of apples. He had tended his few droopy, gnarled trees all year with great care and difficulty, but he was now feeling rather pleased with himself for, by his standards, he had won a good crop. He decided that the Avanos market would probably raise the best prices, and so at three o'clock one morning, Tahir met me outside his house with a donkey and two pannier baskets. Only two baskets were needed, but we filled them to the brim with apples and soon set off in the half-light, across the tarred road to Nevşehir, down into the Valley of the Fairy Chimneys, and out across the stark semi-desert to Avanos. We arrived in good time to set out the baskets in the market place, just as other people were doing, and soon the market was in full swing, with buyers and sellers milling everywhere. Tahir and I sat beside the two panniers, swiping flies away as the sun began to rise past the distant cone of Mount Erciyas. Sometimes Tahir would look up hopefully as people drifted past, perhaps to pick up a sample apple or even to walk off munching one. But eventually a shopkeeper bought some, then another took a few, and at last, after much desultory bickering with potential buyers over the price, all the apples were sold. Sadly Tahir's final takings worked out at less than two pence per kilo—I felt so sorry for my friend, but he simply shrugged, with that 'it is the Will of Allah' look which I had seen so often before. The rewards may have seemed miserable to me, but Tahir would be back in his fields in time for the next year.

I had my second taste of agricultural hardship when Kasim,

the village horse-dealer who had once lent Liz that wonderful stallion, asked me if I could help him with some ploughing, for his own son was ill. We set off in the early morning in a ramshackle cart pulled by a sturdy black horse and laden with a large, heavy, old-fashioned plough. We seemed to travel for miles, bumping down stony paths between people's fields, occasionally pausing to give the horse a rest or to share a melon with the odd farmer working in some nearby plot. We never approached the rows of women whom we sometimes saw, digging and raking and gathering in the encompassing wrap of their white veils—nor did they ever look up at us. Finally Kasim halted, unharnessed the horse, and gathered the plough across his sinewy back. Then off we went across pumpkin fields, through orchards of apples and pears and delicious peaches until at last we reached a tiny patch of rough greyish soil, bound on three sides by rocky cones. One was a ruined church where we ate a light breakfast. Then Kasim hitched the horse to the plough, and began furrowing in neat concentric circles round his precious field. Then came my turn.

Firstly, I had to keep the horse moving forwards, which, as it grew understandably more tired, it was less inclined to do. Secondly, I had to guide the horse by its reins so that the plough would follow a course parallel to its previous circuit. And thirdly, I had, with one hand, to guide the plough through an obstacle course of boulders, holes, sloping ground and hidden roots. Kasim said nothing while I struggled round and round the field, but as I paused for a break in the shade of the cave church I could see for myself where his furrows stopped and my squiggly furrows began. I tried to apologise, but Kasim merely wiped a grimy hand across his brow and smiled at my willingness to try. I may have done a poor job, but I had won another friend.

By lunchtime the field was ploughed to Kasim's satisfaction, so we tramped back to the cart, hitched the horse up, and set off back to Ortahisar, arriving there in mid-afternoon. We had spent eight hours just tilling a scrubby patch of earth no bigger than a golfing green. It seemed such a sad waste of man's energy and care to me, but like Tahir, Kasim would, I knew, take up the struggle again and again, continually finding more reserves of perseverance and will-power which I knew I did not even like to think about.

Summer seemed to be the only time in the year when the village men-folk would, not without some reluctance, leave their tea-houses and trot off on their donkeys to the fields. Man-power was needed during the crucial time of tending and harvesting, when even the men had to admit that the labour involved would be too much for their normally uncomplaining women. Indeed with the arrival of summer, a sort of transformation took place in the village, and a peculiar prosperity seemed to appear. Any walk round Ortahisar's narrow back-streets would reveal showers of gorgeous geraniums growing in profusion from balconies where for most of the year only the washing hung, and any peek through an open courtyard door would show orangy-brown apricots now lying sliced open on innumerable flat roofs, soaking in the sunshine before being cellophane-wrapped for export to Britain. Lorries now began to appear in the car park in front of the inn, bringing cargoes of lemons and grapefruit up from the south coast for preservation in Ortahisar's underground storage vaults. A few men were even employed to drill out some new rock cellars, which they did in about two or three days with pneumatic drills—the Christian monks used to take two or three years. A football match was even arranged between a lorry drivers-pneumatic drillers' eleven and the village team, by whom I was elected goalkeeper—we lost 6–2! It took several revenge wins on the domino board before I was able to regain my tarnished reputation.

Summer also saw more market activity. Not only did dolmuş mini-buses ferry pannier baskets and herds of sheep to and from Nevşehir and Avanos, but even in Ortahisar itself, fruit and vegetables began to appear in piles on the main street, guarded by runny-nosed urchins. Melons seemed to be most popular. A camel also appeared in the village, creating a mild stir by its relatively rare appearance, but when next I saw the poor animal, it was gathering flies on a butcher's trestle table—camel meat was a delicacy, I was told.

August meant the beginning of the harvest, and suddenly wheat was everywhere to be seen, being brought in to the village on scores of tumbledown carts and donkey backs, from dozens of tiny, inaccessible plots of land. Most farmers seemed to look for a suitable piece of flat land—many seemed to have claimed territorial rights by having used the same plot for generations—and there the wheat stalks were laid out in a roughly circular pattern. A horse was then used to drag a heavy wooden comb-like implement round and round across this clearing until it seemed that the wheat ears had all been separated from the stalks, which were then taken away. With that the winnowing began. I spent many fascinated moments watching one farmer tossing the grain up in the air with a wooden pitchfork so that the chaff landed in one pile and the grain in another—rather a risky business should there be a sudden gust of wind, I thought. I did see a solitary combine harvester parked in the car-park by the inn, but I never saw it being used—Tahir told me that most fields were too small, and the access tracks too narrow and rough for such a monster-like machine. People still preferred, it seemed, the timeless certainty of man-power.

Relative prosperity was also brought to Ortahisar by tourism—a difficult pill for many to swallow, but a boon to many more. On a good day there might be as many as ten or twelve foreign cars parked outside the inn, which meant ten guiding opportunities, ten dinners in the village restaurant, and ten more glasses of tea in one of Ortahisar's tea-shops. Postcards and guide-books continued to sell well, and even old Faik, with his antique shop near the 'castle', began to look happier as his trade in Byzantine coins (only some of which were fake, and he did not know which they were) began to improve.

On one occasion, Faik really out-shone himself as an antique merchant. I was supervising the scrubbing of the inn when I was called one August evening to see a fantastic collection of flintlock muskets which Faik had somehow procured—apparently because of my interest in weapons. I never really found out where they came from, for Faik's Turkish was really only a mumble, worsened by a stutter, but I did prick up my ears at 'Kurdistan'. When

I asked if the guns came from Kurdistan, he nodded happily, so I supposed that they must have come from there—I had helped Faik too often for him to try to cheat me. The guns really were magnificent pieces. There were four of them—museum exhibits really—all fully five to six feet long, and exquisitely carved and painstakingly inlaid with miniature pieces of mother-of-pearl and ribbons of silver and gold—not the copper wire used by the antique gun dealers in Istanbul's bazaar. As I handled these wonderful weapons, I kept thinking of the simple tribesmen who perhaps had made them, and indeed used them. Did they know that they had created works of art, or was this craft simply an everyday job to them? Then I recalled the bazaar's illicit underground traffic in modern automatic weapons—many of these were bound ultimately for Kurdistan, where political and bandit needs were keeping alive the demand for arms. In a way, it was a pity, for with factories churning out the rifles now wanted by the Kurds, the craftsmen who had created these extraordinary old muskets would now be long out of work.

Faik wanted £30 for each gun—a very small sum for such treasures—but I simply could not raise the cash for even one musket from the meagre remains of my original £250 award and, rather disappointed, both at having failed to sell anything, and for having failed to find me a suitable souvenir, Faik put the guns away. No doubt they would wind up being sold to some whistle-stop tourist in Istanbul, where the price would be doubled and the artistic and ethnological value of the weapons would be forgotten.

Big Mustafa, who had also noticed my interest in weapons, was next to produce one for sale. He first approached me in the restaurant where, with a conspiratorial whisper from the side of his mouth, he called me over to his table. 'Antique guns!' he hissed urgently into my ear. So off we went to see what he had procured. Mustafa lived in a typical village house with a flat roof and a courtyard, behind whose high walls he carefully unwrapped—a rusty, much-repaired old shotgun! It had its interests, I suppose, for it was at least an old-fashioned percussion-cap weapon, loaded like a musket by ramming the powder and ammunition down its double barrels, which were French—but as an antique it was rubbish. The problem was, how was I to react to Big Mustafa, hovering over me with a face half menacing, half hopeful?

'It's rubbish!' I cried. Mustafa's face gradually assumed a mask of bewilderment, tinged with a touch of faked anger.

'What! Rubbish! Are you saying that this gun, which I have used for years is *rubbish*?'

'Well . . .' I paused, thinking of something better to say. 'Does it work?'

'Of course!' he roared, waving the gun all over the place. 'What's more, it's loaded!'

'Then unload it!' I shrieked.

Mustafa looked puzzled, but obediently drew out the ram-rod, which was a piece of cane with a cork-screw attached to the end. Pushing this down one barrel, he began twiddling it until, with a look of recognition he seemed to catch something with the hook, and pulled out a large rag—the first wad. Then tipping the gun up, he shook out the ammunition, which was an amazing assortment of bent nails, pins, bits of lead and gravel. Then after more twiddling, the second rag appeared, to be followed, to my horror, by a load of black powder—perhaps the most combustible and dangerous of all gunpowders, especially if home-made!

'See! It *was* loaded!' beamed Mustafa. 'Do you want to fire it too?'

'No, no!' I cried. 'Things like that should be banned from Ortahisar!'

'Why?' asked Mustafa, bewildered. 'It's a very old gun.'

'It's not really very old!'

'Yes it is—my father used it!' said Mustafa, his eyebrows furrowing menacingly.

'Well, even that would only make it fifty or sixty years old.'

'No, no! It's really Early Ottoman!' said Mustafa.

'Rubbish!' said I.

'Actually, it's pre-Ottoman!' insisted Mustafa.

'Rubbish!'

'Really, it's Byzantine!' cried Mustafa.

'Rubbish!'

'*It's Roman!*' pleaded Mustafa, as I fell about laughing.

In the end, just to have a souvenir of Big Mustafa and his devious dealings, I exchanged the gun for a shirt, a small bottle of Codeine for Mustafa's 'headache', the promise of an introduction to the next attractive female tourist to dine at the village restaurant, and £2.

I never really found out the extent to which Turks actually carried guns—I saw several men using rifles on hunting trips, especially in winter when wolves became a problem—but I never actually saw any pistols stuck into trouser waists, though I did hear shooting on occasions, sometimes during distant wedding revelries or after a night of drinking. Nevertheless, there was a widely reported press story of a bus which was totally incinerated in a crash—seventeen revolvers were found among the charred bodies of the passengers.

As August wore on, it became clear that the Ürgüp–Ortahisar–Nevşehir area was actually beginning to experience a modest tourist boom. A motel appeared at Ürgüp, with a swimming pool (which was unfortunately filled with stagnant water), and colourful umbrellas now shaded the occasional table and chair. A large hotel was opened at Nevşehir, and more whistle-stop buses began to appear in Ortahisar. Some prices began to rise in Ürgüp, and neighbouring inns began to put on synthetic folk-music evenings. Soon I was beginning to fear that the very core of the region might, like so many other places, become polluted by the brashness of tourism.

Fortunately, although the outer appearance of Ortahisar began to alter slightly, the core survived. The four or five military conscripts who constituted the village police force now spent much time erecting telegraph wires and electric cables, which soon made it almost impossible to photograph the main street without including a lattice-work of unsightly wires. A new teahouse was opened, and a new antique shop also appeared to rival that of Faik. A shiny new dolmuş appeared one day beside the inn, bought by the proud driver of a previously ramshackle old van—that now made three dolmuş drivers shouting out their destinations in the early morning. At the same time, a group of men arrived back from Holland, where they had been employed as textile workers. They brought with them many bright new dresses and shirts, and for a while these stood out conspicuously among the multi-patched hand-me-downs which most people wore, until they too became grubby and patched, and were absorbed into the village landscape.

These changes were but ephemeral, however, for they never really penetrated the day-to-day lives of most people. The women still trudged off daily to the fields, the storage of grapefruit and lemons went on, the village mayor still drove off once a month to plead for better roads and a Middle School from the vilayet officials in Kayseri, and the innkeeper still forgot to replace the toilet paper and the sheets in the hotel. Tahir still struggled to impose on Ortahisar the benefits which his father had begun to introduce, and when I left, he was still the only male villager who combed his hair and did not wear a skip cap.

Eventually, with time now beginning to run out, I decided that I would try to photograph some of the women whom I had befriended during the previous year. As an initial step I consulted Tahir, who asked his mother if she would agree to being photographed. To begin with, she was reluctant, but after I had complimented her on her cooking, and had presented her with a tiny embroidered handkerchief from Scotland, she posed for me in her courtyard, where no one else could see her. It was a great moment for me, as I pressed the button on my camera—perhaps the greatest compliment that I could have been given by Mrs Köse. Tahir also asked his two little nieces if they would agree to being photographed, but they solemnly shook their heads and ran off. They were enticed back again by a stick of Brighton Rock, and eventually they agreed to having their backs photographed—which suited me, for they had lovely hair, done in about forty long pigtails which hung down to their waists. And by thus cajoling and bargaining, Tahir and I also managed to persuade his sister, and later a couple of her friends, to be photographed. But there my successes stopped, for although I was well known and liked by many village women, I had, even after a year, still not become sufficiently close to them to be allowed to take any pictures. Here too, perhaps, was evidence that Ortahisar's real core was changing little, in spite of tourism and some prosperity.

Eventually, I decided that I would have to leave Ortahisar. I spent the next few days feeling depressed about this, for I had grown to love the distant braying of donkeys and the sun rising from behind Mount Erciyas, but I kept myself occupied until the last moment, writing another hopeless letter off to Germany begging compensation for the loss of someone's hand in a machine accident, giving last-minute tips to my trainee tourist guides, and even taking one British couple round Göreme myself. I spent that last fee on a handful of Byzantine coins, but they turned out to be mostly fakes—it seemed that I had failed, at least as an archaeologist! I also drew a pen-and-ink sketch of the 'castle' for the owner of the village pastry shop—he was so pleased with it that he hung it up in a gilt frame in his shop, but he soon retired to be a farmer, and it now hangs in his own house, looking rather out of place among magnificent carpets and fiery-red geraniums.

I gave the last of my medicines to Yaşar bey, the village mayor—much to the annoyance of Big Mustafa who had hoped to acquire what was left. But by now I knew better than to give them to the biggest scoundrel in the village. At least they would be fairly distributed by Yaşar bey. Then I packed my enormous black trunk and the rest of my suitcases, leaving only some clean clothes at the top for a few days in Istanbul, where I wanted to see Merih and the Algans—perhaps I would even manage a little relaxed swimming before taking the Orient Express home.

On the night before my departure, a great party was held in the restaurant, where a tremendous meal had been prepared by Ali, the chef. Someone appeared with a sas, and as the piles of food began to shrink, and the wine began to flow more freely, so the music and the laughter and the banter became louder and happier, until the room was whirling and the happiness was flowing through my blood. Big Mustafa was there, maintaining a jovial smile to the last in spite of having missed my medicines. Kemal the hunchback was there with another bottle, insisting on more toasts. Old Abdulla was there asking forgiveness for having scrounged so many medicines from me. Kasin the horse-dealer was there. Yaşar bey the mayor appeared, and so did the teachers from the little school, and the librarian from Ortahisar's wonderful little library. Tahir appeared with a bowl of my favourite grape sauce from his mother, and together we all danced and finger-snapped until the sas-players could play no more.

As I looked round that sea of sweating, happy, friendly faces, I knew that this was a picture that I would carry in my mind for ever. But what, I wondered, would be my lasting impressions of the village itself? Would they be of the sights and sounds, like the braying donkeys and the flat roofs and the apricots and the clinking of tea-glasses? Or would they be of the things that I had done, in trying to improve the little inn, or trying to plough a field, or learning to guide people round the Fairy Chimneys? Or would my impressions be of the things which I had experienced —perhaps only because I had now mastered Turkish, and had been prepared to join the village in *its* way of life instead of introducing it to mine—experiences which had humbled me, enlightened me, saddened me, or perhaps made me more understanding? What also had I given *to* this community which had so willingly opened its doors to an infidel? Had my medicines helped, or would the future lack of them only seem more obvious? Had the inn's new image helped, or would tourism now swamp Ortahisar? Had I helped the villagers to understand something of the West, or had they seen how spoiled and ungrateful were many Europeans? Had I been a credit to my father or to my mother, also remembered with such affection by the villagers?

But then I was snapped out of my day-dreaming by a hearty smack on the back from Big Mustafa.

'Come on Craig bey!' he roared. 'I've plenty more wine where this came from!' And I looked round happily at all those faces, smiling at the *doktoroğlu*. What a party we had! The dancing and singing went on far into the night. Someone outside started shooting off his revolver and had to be quietened. Someone else complained that he couldn't see into the restaurant for the steamed-up windows, and finally clambered in through the kitchen window. . . . Ortahisar had not seen a night like this for months! Neither had I!

But the next morning, before the first minaret call, I was gone.

Appendix 1 The Latest Word on Carpets

The rapid commercialization of carpet-selling in Turkey has led to unprecedented changes in the quality, style, origin and materials used in many carpets. So many changes have occurred, even since going to press, that a new summary is now needed.

At present, the general quality of carpets is declining, while prices in city bazaars are increasing, faster than in the villages from where most carpets originate. Carpets of wool or silk on either silk, cotton or wool backing, are giving way to wool-and-silk mixtures, and inferior wools usually taken from dead animals, thus producing a high proportion of hard, rough, and brittle carpets. When compared to the older type, knotted with wool taken only from the choicest parts of live lambs, the difference is immediate, but with fewer good carpets left in the bazaars, the contrast is not easily found and the chances of being sold a poor-quality piece, for lack of comparison, are increased.

Until recently, colours were manufactured by village women, using walnuts for brown, saffron for yellow, tulip petals for reds, vegetables or pine needles for greens, indigo for blue, and so on. Today, between seventy and ninety per cent of all carpets sold in the Grand Bazaar at Istanbul are synthetically coloured, which eventually leads to dyes running during the washing of carpets, or fading in sunlight—flaws not found with vegetable dyes. Sadly, some villagers are no longer making carpets simply for their own needs, but have turned to mass production, with squads of young girls working at the looms all the year round; unfortunately, vegetable dyes have been among the first of the traditional qualities to disappear.

The number of the knots has also decreased, from an average of about eighty or ninety tufts per square cm. for an ordinary piece, to a present figure of about forty-two per square cm.

All this has necessitated a reappraisal of where the best carpets now come from. Kayseri, once a celebrated area, is now generally decried, for its quality has declined, the colours are synthetic, and there is much copying of the styles of other regions. The current areas of highest quality are Bursa, Konya, Sivas, Bunyan, and Gördes.

Regions to avoid include Kayseri (except for older pieces), and Isparta.

Although this saddening trend is increasing, the carpets sold by Mehmet Ali are generally still of quality. Ara, the salesman, maintains this quality both by avoiding carpets from areas such as Kayseri, and by bartering for carpets with household goods such as washing machines or refrigerators, highly prized by Anatolia's poor villagers, who will part with high-quality family-made carpets in exchange. Buying a carpet with a fridge also keeps the price down to a competitive level with the mass-produced low-quality pieces sold elsewhere. But even then, Ara does not return to the same Anatolian family for ten years, lest they too turn to mass production.

Finally, when handling carpets, the following points must now *always* be considered: how *old* is the piece? (the older the better); from which area does it *originate*? what is its *quality*? (the cut of wool, the type of dyes used, the number of knotting flaws, etc.); and how *rare* is its design? Any carpet which measures up well to these four essential criteria will be not only an heirloom, but a priceless piece of Turkish workmanship.

Appendix 2

Notes on the Rock Churches

These notes, on the best surviving churches in Cappadocia, are the 'academic' results of my stay in Turkey. About eighty-five churches and chapels have survived erosion and vandalism, some in better condition than others now, but all with significant material for interested travellers and historians. These notes should also be of use to readers, who may feel that the text has not enough detailed information.

THE GÖREME COLLECTION

Aynali (The Mirror Church). Slightly apart from the main group of churches, and in reasonable condition. Has some disfigured paintings, possibly of the tenth century.

Barbara (Chapel of Saint Barbara). Situated in the heart of Göreme. Noted mainly for its early ochre decorations. Cruciform plan with a *Christus* in the apse. May have been a baptismal chapel. Dated eighth century.

Çarkali (Church of the Sandals). So called because of a set of footprints carved in the floor of the southern transept, said to be a copy of those in the Church of the Ascension, Jerusalem. Cross plan with central cupola, but irregular shape. Artistic themes are the Nativity, the Crucifixion, and the Ascension. Note also the Hospitality of Abraham showing Abraham with Sara. The Transfiguration scene shows Jesus with James and the Prophets: this is an unusual scene. Church is Constantinople influence, eleventh century.

Daniel (Church of Daniel). In poor condition, but some paintings survive. Tenth century?

Elmali (Apple Church). Very famous: one of the 'Churches with Columns'. Note: no passage between the sanctuary and the Chapel of Prothesis, and the narthex has disappeared with erosion. All columns are original. Of the scenes, note especially the Betrayal, the Crucifixion, the Baptism, the Transfiguration, and the Nativity. Colours are bright; some ochre appears from underneath. Influenced by Constantinople. Eleventh-century work.

Eustace (Church of St Eustace). Situated apart from the central group.

In fair condition but has suffered from damp and vandalism. Date uncertain.

Firketan (Firketan Church). Could be very old, but the date unknown. Situated apart from the rest in a gorge. Mainly red ochre painting, in zigzags and geometric patterns. Influences in the architecture uncertain. Outer façade probably more recent.

Jerphanion (church found by Père Jerphanion). Situated apart from the main group. In poor condition.

Kiliçlar (Church of the Swords). Situated apart, and has four large columns. Note scenes of the Benediction of the Apostles, Pentecost, the Nativity, and paintings from the childhood of Jesus. Fair condition, but date unknown.

Karanlik (The Dark Church). Cappadocia's most famous church, and one of the 'Churches with Columns'. Lit by only one window but the paintings are superb: too many frescoes to enumerate, but the most magnificent are the Benediction of the Apostles, the Annunciation and the Hospitality of Abraham, all in the narthex; at least one Christus, and scenes of John the Baptist, in the central aisle; an image of Jesus in the right-hand aisle; the Journey to Jerusalem, the Nativity, the Baptism, the Transfiguration, the Entry into Jerusalem, the Last Supper, the Betrayal, the Crucifixion, and The Ascension, all in the Naos. The Last Supper and the Betrayal are the two most famous scenes in Cappadocia. Church's plan is irregular and includes a Naos built of four columns, a narthex, and an acrosoleum. Constantinople influence, eleventh century.

Miriam Ana (Church to the Virgin Mary). Lesser known and situated apart from the main group. Some paintings, but damaged. Influences unknown but could date from tenth century.

Ninazan (The Ninazan Church). Set quite far from Göreme and is quite extensively damaged by erosion. Nevertheless, some fair paintings survive for the moment. Main scene still preserved is the Nativity. Possible southern influence. Tenth century?

Sakli (The Hidden Church). Situated near the above, but much more difficult to find. Constructed with a narthex and three apses, and has a double nave achieved by a dividing arcade. Note especially scenes of St John in the Desert, the Crucifixion, the Presentation (strongly Hellenistic) and lesser moments in the life of Christ. Lower walls damaged by dampness. General style of the church possibly Mesopotamian. Paintings dated twelfth to thirteenth century, and construction anywhere between ninth to twelfth centuries.

Theodore (Church of St Theodore). Possibly a funerary chapel, but the church also has scenes of St George and St Theodore. Several graves in the narthex however. Influence is uncertain, but the church dates from the tenth century.

Tokali (The Buckle Church). From which relics were stolen before the Museum authorities got there. The church is in two parts: the Old Tokali is Syro-Palestinian in influence and depicts scenes from the life of St Basil. The New Tokali, consisting of lateral apses and chapels, is sombre and less interesting. The entire church contains the full cycle of the events in the life of Jesus. Old Tokali's date uncertain, but possibly eighth century, the New Tokali is tenth century.

Theodokas (Church of St Theodokas). Lies apart from the main group. In fair condition but little is known of the date or influence.

Yilanli (The Snake Church). Situated in the centre of Göreme, this church is of the eighth century, having extensive red ochre decoration. Later scenes depict full-length portraits of the Emperor Constantine and his wife Helene, St Enoyfrios, St George killing a dragon (sometimes confused with St Prokopion) and St Theodore on a red horse. Influence mainly Byzantine.

Göreme has several more chapels, mainly used as funerary and private churches. There are also two monasteries, one convent, and at least three refectories, one of which has been partially rebuilt.

CHURCHES NEAR GÖREME

Yeni (The New Church). Situated at *Çavuşin*, and sometimes called the Church with Columns, there is little left save interesting bandeaux on the windows, of Syrian style. Date unknown.

Aci (The Church of St John). Sometimes called the Church of St Joan, perhaps by mistake. Portrait of St John and various scenes from the life of Jesus. Colours well preserved. Situated close to the village of Çavuşin. Date unknown: tenth century?

Güllü Church. Situated beside the above, and possibly once a funerary chapel. No paintings of interest, but a few ochre sketches.

Kizil Çukur (Church in the district of Kizil Çukur). Badly defaced paintings in this church, which is also very difficult to find. Date unknown, but possibly eleventh century.

Üzümlü (Grape Church). Also situated in the region of Kizil Çukur —a district close to Göreme which is a maze of impenetrable gullies. The church is badly damaged but the main motif of bunches of grapes still remains on the ceiling. Much vandalism.

Meskender Church (in the same area). Also badly destroyed.

Two chapels also survive among the caves of Zilve, but these are badly defaced and worn. Interesting bandeaux however.

THE ORTAHISAR COLLECTION

Cambasli (The Cambasli Church). Situated literally below the village 'castle' at Ortahisar, and difficult to find. At one time two churches, but now linked together. The original church in the usual cruciform with central cupola. Frescoes of Jesus, the Virgin Mary, Constantine and Helene, and all in fairly good condition: not much vandalism by comparison, and colours preserved. Dated tenth century?

Balkan (The Balkan Church). Difficult to find, and much broken down by erosion. Few paintings remain save for some decoration in one cupola. Disappointing. Date uncertain.

Saracik (Saracik Church). Close to the above, and equally disappointing, having only a few ochre paintings.

Pancarlik (The Pancarlik Church). To the east of Ortahisar, and very hard to find without a guide. Interesting church, with sculpted columns and friezes, moulded bandeaux on the walls, and unusual apse steps. These and the paintings much vandalised, however. Brash colours, mainly browns, greens, and ochres. Date uncertain, but influence may be Syrian.

Kepez Kilisler (The Kepez Churches). Much destroyed by erosion, very difficult to find, but with character and serenity. Paintings darkened and defaced, but appear to be scenes from the life of Mary the Mother of Jesus. Main church was cruciform, but with double nave and triple apse. Unusual design but influence and date unknown.

Tavşanli Kilisler (The Tavşanli or Rabbit Churches). Guide needed to find this pair of chapels. Paintings defaced and eroded, but what survives is interesting. Note predominant blue colouring and secular scenes of animals, rare in Cappadocia. Date uncertain.

Kara (The Black Church). As the name suggest, very dark inside, with sooted frescoes. Disappointing. Possible southern influences in architecture however.

Halaş Deresi (Hospital at Halaş Deresi). Not far from Ortahisar, and not too difficult to find. Consists of an underground hospital and associated chapel. Columned chambers, and quite spacious, but little decoration save red ochre designs. Date unknown.

Hidravat (Hidravat Church). Near the hospital, but more obscure. Poor decorations and architecture. Date uncertain.

There are also two rock 'castles' in the village of Ortahisar, known as the Sağ Kale and the Isaak Kale. Dating them is impossible. A former prison also exists above the road to Göreme.

AT GÜLSEHIR

Karşi (usually called St John's Church). Originally on two floors, but the former wooden floor gone and the steps very worn. Paintings dark and not restored. Church dates from thirteenth century, and as such is very rare. Some vandalism. Influence unclear.

Two more chapels of little note exist nearby. Also the *Açik Saray* or Open Palace: this is a collection of chapels and underground tunnels of unknown date. Very disappointing because of vandalism.

THE PERISTREMA COLLECTION

The Ala Kilise (The Mottled Church). Near village of Bellisirma. Has impressive façade of broad porch and three-tier arches. Is now used as store-house and mill (using old Byzantine mill-stone), but frescoes still survive in SW. chamber, including the Entry into Jerusalem and the Last Supper (badly defaced). Note also the Three Israelites from Book of Daniel being thrown into the furnace, and scenes from the Burial of St Mary the Egyptian. Also the Descent into Hell, the Five Armenian Martyrs, the Persian Martyrs, and four of the Seven Sleepers of Ephesus. Some very rare frescoes in this church, several of high artistic merit. Church plan is cruciform with central cupola and later cupolas in the transepts. Influence is eleventh-century Byzantine.

Direkli (Church with Pillars). Church is cruciform with triple apse and central cupola on square pillars. Very dark because only one small window. Note Christus above central apse, flanked by St Michael and

St Gabriel. In the same apse, also Christ in Judgement, flanked by the Virgin Mary, separated by medallions of Peter and Paul. Dated by inscription as late tenth-century Byzantine.

Bahattin Samanliği (Bahattin's Granary Church). Placed near the above. Smaller, with cradle vault and two niches on north wall, three niches on south wall of which the central one is the door. Walls are thin and church in danger of collapse. Twenty-three scenes from the life of Christ and a few of saints. Tones, once bright and colourful, now dark. Byzantine tenth to eleventh century.

St George's Church. Situated a short distance upstream from Bellisirma, and so called because of five scenes of George and the dragon. The only known frescoes in Cappadocia from later thirteenth century, and therefore of great importance. Dated 1283–95: Byzantine.

Karagedik (St Ermolaos Church). Built of trachyte and brick but badly damaged by falling boulders and vandalism. What frescoes survive are of the Martyrdom of St George. Date unknown.

Yilanli (The Snake Church). Roughly cruciform with a small transept window and a funerary chapel in the narthex. Scenes in the vestibule include unique Burial of St Mary the Egyptian with St Zosimus laying her in the sarcophagus by means of a ramp. In the narthex are Christ in Judgement, the Twenty-four Elders, the Forty Martyrs of Sebastea. The Twenty-four Elders otherwise found only in St Peter without the Walls at Rome, and the Church of St Simeon at Aswan, Egypt. The scene is therefore very rare indeed. Rare presentation of the Last Supper, and an unusual Last Judgement. Colours in this church are very harsh, except for one shade of pink; figures are rigid and formal. Date uncertain: Syrian or Egyptian Coptic influence.

Sümbüllü (The Church of the Lilies). This church, perhaps once a monastery, resembles Göreme style. Paintings, though damaged by damp, are of a very high quality. Note especially the Annunciation, the Presentation in the Temple, and the Dormition. Byzantine influence of the tenth to eleventh centuries.

Ağaç Alti (The Church beneath the Tree). Small domed church with door where an apse once was. Crude draughtsmanship but fine harmonious painting. Note especially Christ by the bed of His Mother, with St John nearby: Jesus would seem to be holding the soul of the

Virgin in His hand, for He is carrying a doll. The Dormition has no equal in Cappadocian rock painting. Fresco figures are all too similar: e.g. the Three Magi. Lettering would suggest date as early as possible sixth century: no later than tenth. Strong Arab and Syrian influence.

Pürenli (Church of the Terraces). A small chapel with only a few, poorly-drawn frescoes hurriedly created. Nevertheless pleasing but similar to styles found at Göreme. Date uncertain.

Kolar (Church of the Sweet Smells). Apse missing due to landslide, but many paintings survive. Note especially the Ascension, the Burning of the Three Israelites in the Furnace (their names are written in Babylonian instead of the Greek form: Ananias, Misael and Azarias, which is unique in Byzantine iconography according to Dr Thierry). Note also several scenes from the life of Christ. Hurriedly painted church with limited colours. Possible Syrian influence but date unknown.

Eğri Taş (The Crooked Rock Church). This is one of the most important churches in the gorge, with several rare frescoes of high artistic quality. Was previously a church above a funerary chamber, but the wooden floor long gone. Paintings defaced and some scenes difficult to identify. The best include a very rare Virgin at the Well, the Visitation, the Annunciation, the Nativity, the Coming of the Magi (unusual because they wear Persian trousers, and because they are depicted as being old, middle-aged, and young), a scene of the Denial of Peter, the Women at the Tomb, the Entry into Jerusalem, the Flight into Egypt (also unusual because the fresco depicts Joseph, Mary, and Jesus accompanied by Joseph's traditional two sons by his first marriage), a very rare Garden of Gethsemene, and an equally rare Washing of Jesus' Feet. The frescoes have strong resemblances to both Mozarabic and Merovingian illuminations, and to eighth- to ninth-century Roman mosaics. Church was dedicated to the Mother of God and was donated by someone called Christopher, who was a *Turmarch*—roughly a general. The frescoes are very individual and interesting and the colours, though lacking variety, are skilfully used. Strong Syro-Palestinian influence and very old: fifth to tenth century.

There are also three monasteries in the collection; the first at Selima, and the second at Yaprak Hisar, both at the lower end of the ravine, and the third at the *Karanlik Kale* (the Dark Tower) which lies opposite the Kolar and Pürenli Churches. This later monastery has a few Iconoclastic decorations, but the first two are more interesting. Three unpainted churches exist between the Yaprak Hisar monastery and Bellisirma, and another two lie between the Karagedik Church and the Snake Church, but these have long lost their frescoes.

I wish to acknowledge the considerable use made of M. and Mme Thierry's book in the compilation of the section on Peristrema: although I have visited the valley twice, the Thierrys reign as the undisputed experts on its churches.

ESKI GÜMÜS

The Monastery. Entry by a tunnel to a hewn courtyard, with the monastery rooms leading off on all sides. Façade is similar to several at Göreme and Peristrema.

The Church. Consists of a roughly-cut exo-narthex leading from the courtyard into a well-hewn narthex with careful barrel vaulting and a blind arcade on each wall; and the church itself, with an eastern apse flanked by niches, an arcaded recess, and two tombs to the left, entered by an arch. The frescoes in the narthex are: The Virgin and Child flanked by the archangels Gabriel and Michael, several Maltese crosses, and a fine Latin cross. Church decorations are: the Apostles, the Fathers of the Church, Christ Pantocrator, the Virgin and Child (particularly beautiful), the Annunciation, portraits of SS Stephen and John, the Nativity and the Presentation (revealed after restoration), the Adoration of the Magi, and the Washing of the Child. The narthex paintings in particular are reminiscent of Göreme, but because they have all been so long protected by soot and candle-grease, the paintings are considered to be excellent examples of middle-Byzantine art. Some carvings in local marble and fragments of Corinthian column have also been found. Monastery dated A.D. 1050–1150.

The Upstairs Room. The fascinating diversion of an unknown monk in the form of frescoes depicting scenes from Aesop's Fables. Details given in Chapter Nine of this book.

THE SOĞANLI COLLECTION

Ak (The White Church). Much defaced simple cruciform church. Disappointing and damaged.

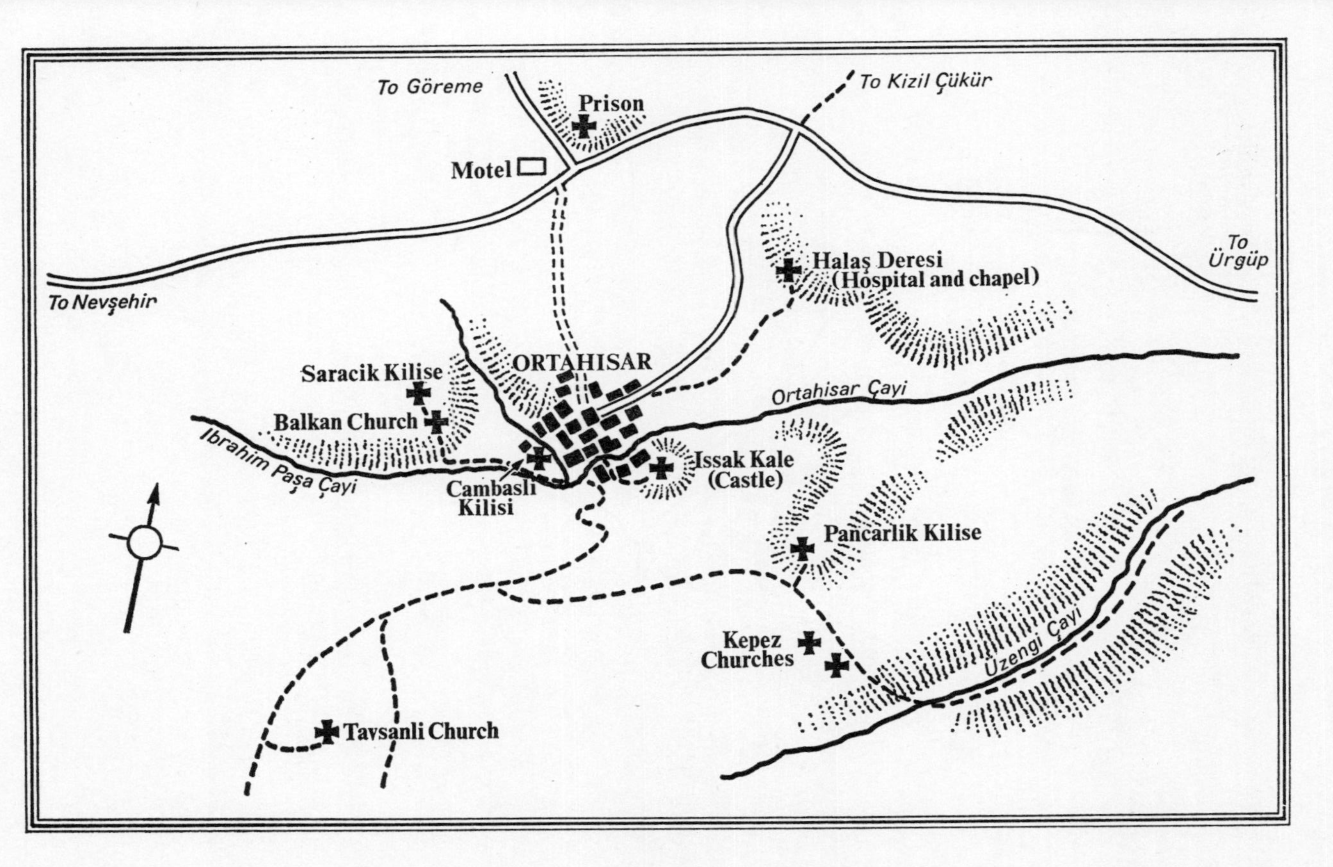

To Göreme
Prison
To Kizil Çukür
Motel
To Ürgüp
Halaş Deresi
(Hospital and chapel)
To Nevşehir
ORTAHISAR
Saracik Kilise
Balkan Church
Ortahisar Çayi
Ibrahim Paşa Çayi
Issak Kale
(Castle)
Cambasli
Kilisi
Pancarlik Kilise
Kepez
Churches
Üzengi Çayi
Tavsanli Church

Ortahisar

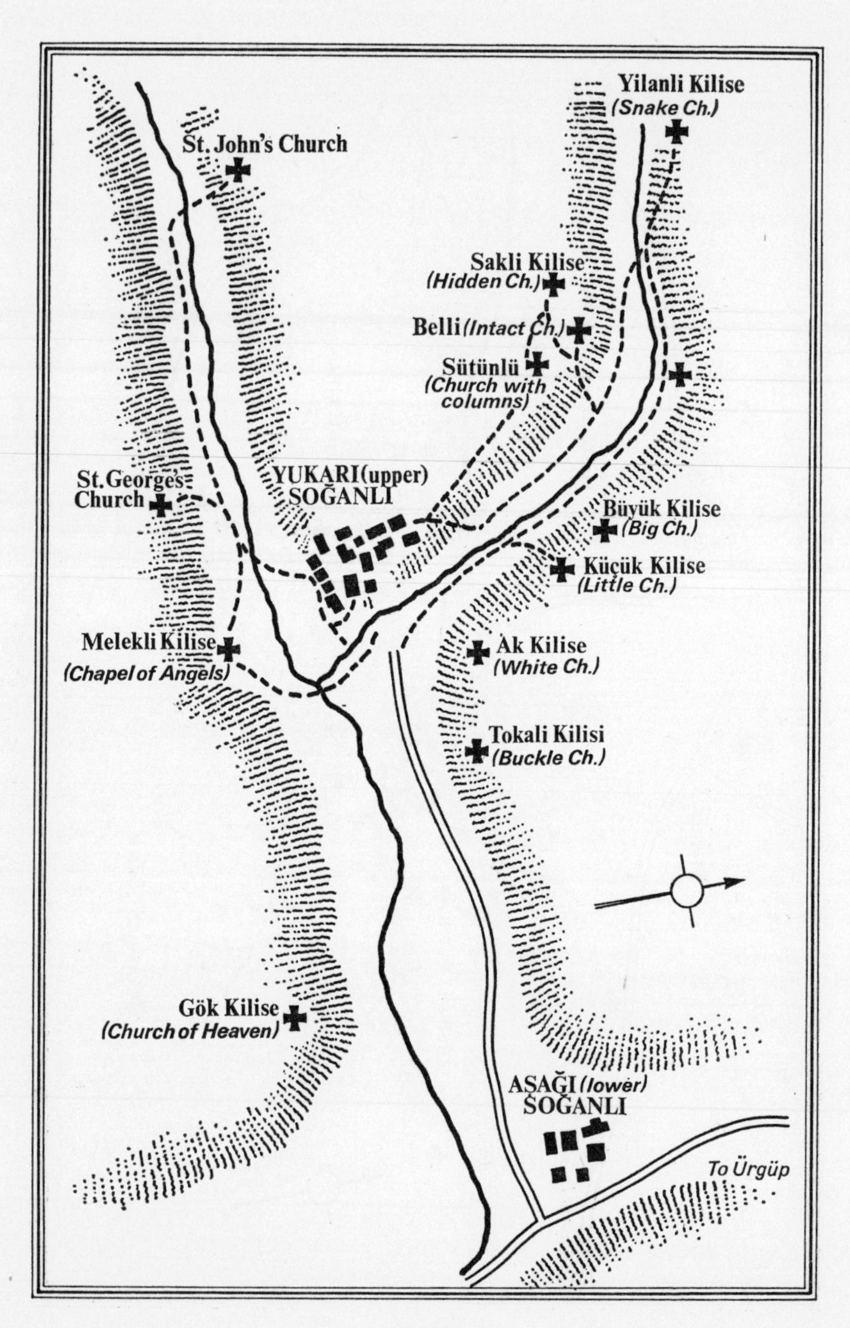
Yilanli Kilise
(Snake Ch.)
St. John's Church
Sakli Kilise
(Hidden Ch.)
Belli (Intact Ch.)
Sütünlü
(Church with
columns)
St. George's
Church
YUKARI (upper)
SOĞANLI
Büyük Kilise
(Big Ch.)
Küçük Kilise
(Little Ch.)
Melekli Kilise
(Chapel of Angels)
Ak Kilise
(White Ch.)
Tokali Kilisi
(Buckle Ch.)
Gök Kilise
(Church of Heaven)
ASAĞI (lower)
SOĞANLI
To Ürgüp

Soğanli

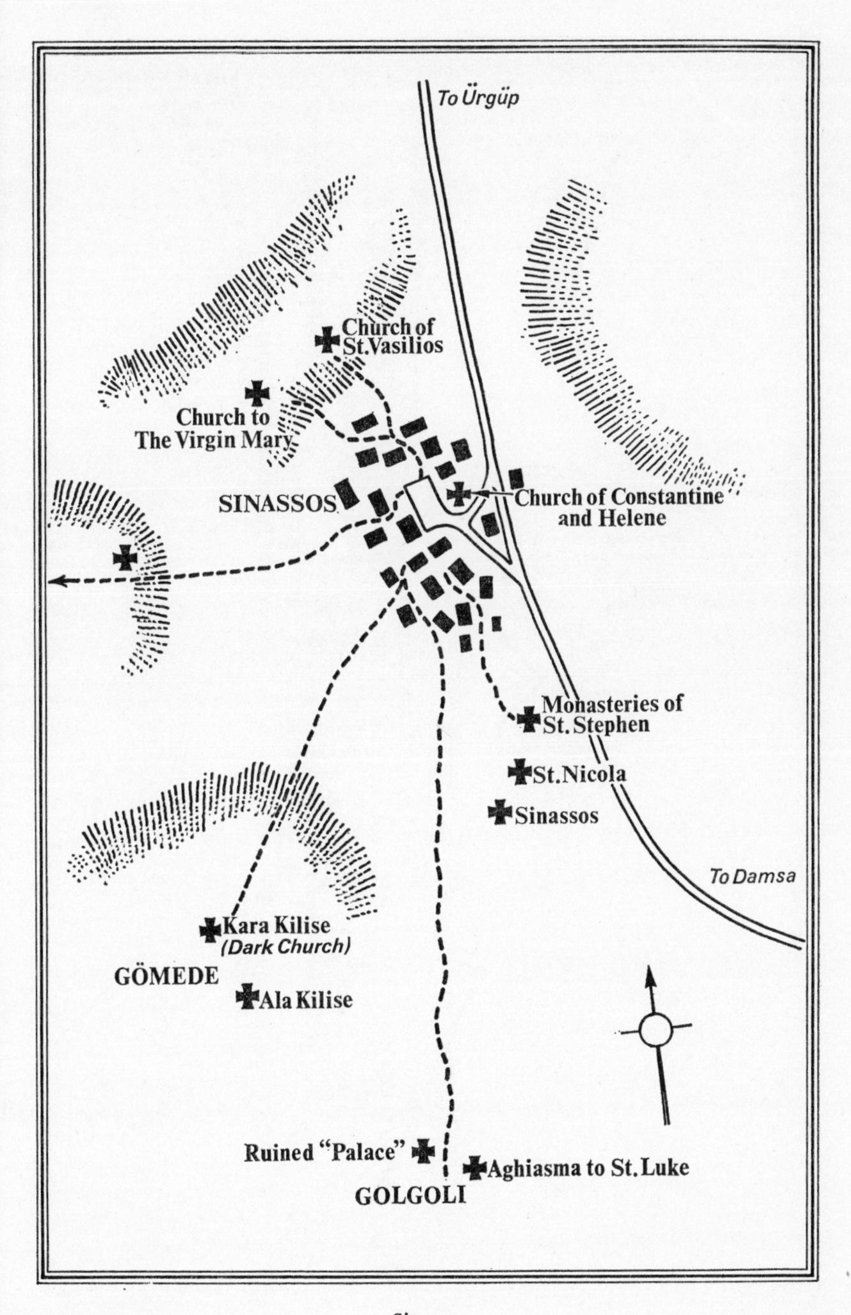
To Ürgüp
Church of St.Vasilios
Church to The Virgin Mary
SINASSOS
Church of Constantine and Helene
Monasteries of St. Stephen
St.Nicola
Sinassos
To Damsa
Kara Kilise
(Dark Church)
GÖMEDE
Ala Kilise
Ruined "Palace"
Aghiasma to St. Luke
GOLGOLI

Sinassos

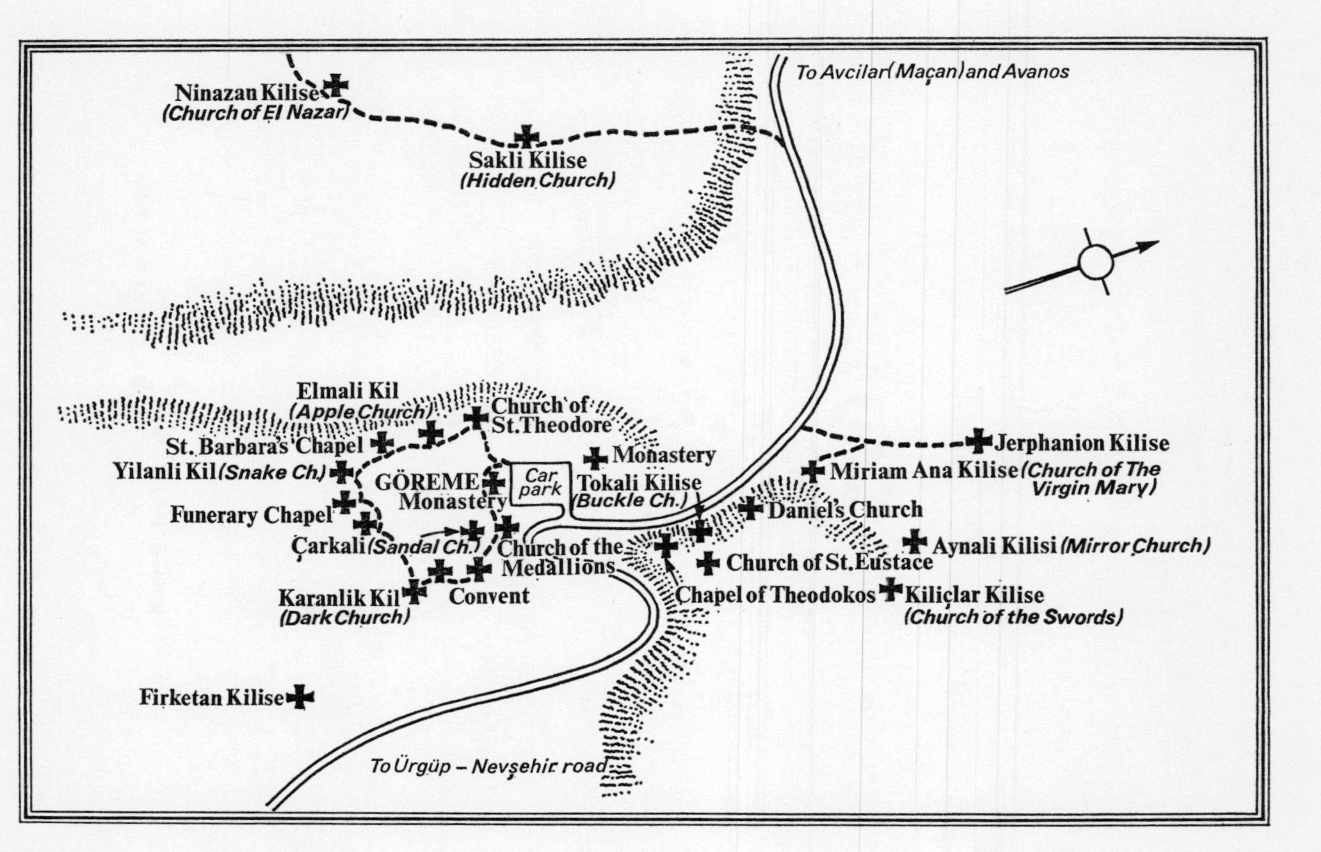

To Avcilar (Maçan) and Avanos
Ninazan Kilise (Church of El Nazar)
Sakli Kilise (Hidden Church)
Elmali Kil (Apple Church)
Church of St. Theodore
St. Barbara's Chapel
Yilanli Kil (Snake Ch.)
GÖREME Monastery
Car park
Monastery
Tokali Kilise (Buckle Ch.)
Funerary Chapel
Çarkali (Sandal Ch.)
Church of the Medallions
Karanlik Kil (Dark Church)
Convent
Jerphanion Kilise
Miriam Ana Kilise (Church of The Virgin Mary)
Daniel's Church
Aynali Kilisi (Mirror Church)
Church of St. Eustace
Chapel of Theodokos
Kiliçlar Kilise (Church of the Swords)
Firketan Kilise
To Ürgüp – Nevşehir road

Göreme

Notes on the Rock Churches

Ballek (The Ballek Church). So named because it lies in the *deresi* or valley of the Ballek Stream. Plan includes two parallel naves with a sanctuary to the right of the first of these. Colours are harsh, being red and green. Paintings much defaced by vandals and destroyed by erosion, revealing older red ochre underneath. Main scenes are of the Crucifixion, the Baptism (with an unusual inclusion of St Zacharius), a portrait of St Oreste on horseback, and a very rare secular scene of a peasant ploughing. Locals claim Armenian influence, but this is doubtful for it appears pure Byzantine. Possibly tenth century.

Belli or *Kubbeli* (The Intact Church). Distinguished by exterior Armenian architecture. Plan is a simple cruciform with a central cupola and a small chapel built into one corner of the cross form. Paintings, applied on to plaster, are damaged by erosion and defaced. Armenian and Byzantine influence, possibly of the tenth century.

Büyük (The Big Church). Larger church of possible tenth- or eleventh-century work. Frescoes, generally in greens and reds, much vandalised and hard to tell individual scenes. Byzantine influence.

Gök (The Church of Heaven). Situated near the mouth of the Soğanli Valley, but I have not yet examined this chapel properly. Paintings are not in good condition, however.

Küçük (The Little Church). Simple cruciform but frescoes unfortunately defaced and dampened. Colours are pleasing: several scenes of (perhaps) the Virgin Mary. Byzantine tenth century?

Melekli (The Chapel of the Angels). Apparently in fair condition, but having only visited this church once, in evening half-light, I cannot really comment further.

Miriam Ana (Church to the Holy Mother). A complicated plan, consisting of a narthex and nave, beyond which and up some steps lie two further burial chambers. Paintings ruined by vandalism but main colours used are reds and greens. The best surviving scene is of the Crucifixion, but it is very similar to others at Göreme. Paintings appear hurried and are not very pleasing. Iconoclastic designs extend into the burial acrosolium beyond.

Chapel to St George. So called because of a scene of a mounted figure who could be St George, but who might be any of the Anatolian soldier saints. Paintings defaced. Byzantine influence.

Church to St John. No apparent reason why the chapel should be to this saint, for there does not appear to be any particularly strong reference to him among the few defaced frescoes surviving.

Sakli (The Hidden Church). In the form of a cross with a central cupola: a very neat church but unfortunately full of fallen rubble which has not been cleared. Few paintings exist and there are only isolated patches of colour. Byzantine tenth to eleventh century.

Sütunlu (The Church with Columns). Three columns remain in this cruciform church. There is also a triple apse, a chamber beyond the door, and an altar to right of door. The church much cluttered by masonry. What paintings survive damage resemble the frescoes of the Old Tokali Kilise at Göreme and may therefore be also of Syro-Palestinian influence. Date uncertain but possibly of tenth century.

Tokali (The Buckle Church). This church better preserved, with a double nave, triple apse, funerary chapel to right of door and four intact columns. Frescoes applied on to rough surface, and are mainly of reds and greens. The church is in surprisingly good condition. Probably Byzantine of the eleventh century.

It is said that there are more churches in the area; namely the so-called *Barbara Church*, a Chapel to *St Eustathius*, and the *Çanavar Church*, but I was unable to trace any of these. The Karabak Monastery is also in the area.

THE SINASSOS COLLECTION

The Church of Constantine and Helene. Situated unobtrusively in the village square. A stone-built church with an outside porch and inside, a nave flanked by aisles, and an apse at the far end. Iconoclastic designs survive on the columns of the nave, and obscure scenes remain in the dome, but there is little else of interest. Dating very difficult: Byzantine style.

Ay Nikola Monastery. Entered by a portal gateway with the monastery's name inscribed above; inside a spacious courtyard with outbuildings. The buildings appear modern, but may be restored or perhaps a small chapel enlarged. White plaster surface everywhere inside with paintings drawn into contrived panels. Main colours are blues, greens and reds: main themes are local saints.

Aya Stefanos (The Monastery of St Stephen). A much-restored building consisting of a number of chapels, many of them with proper pulpits—not common in Cappadocia. Again whitewashed walls, but as elsewhere in Sinassos, they have been defaced by children. Paintings found mainly in panels and on the ceiling.

Sinassos (The Sinassos Monastery). Like the previous two monasteries, the architecture has not been much eroded or destroyed, but the paintings have been vandalised by vicious scars.

Ayos Vasilios (The Monastery of St Vasilios). Built into a cliff-side but entered through a small building from above which leads down a staircase into the church. This is the most impressive monastery in the Sinassos collection, being the best preserved and the most recent (probably). Plan is a double nave, each with its own altar in its own apse. One nave also has a narthex which leads to the staircase. The church, whitewashed and well lit by windows, is very bright: the brash, bright colours of the frescoes are therefore very striking. Frescoes found mainly on the stair walls, in panels on the church walls, and in circular panels on the ceilings. Again the subject matter is generally local, but some portraits more familiar: Constantine and Helene, for example. Dating impossible, for the church may be enlarged or restored. Paintings are modern.

Miriam Ana (Chapel to the Virgin Mary). Situated in the area of *Golgoli*, and dates from the tenth century.

Aghiasma to St Luke. Not far from above chapel but dating is virtually impossible. Still in reasonable condition but hard to find and a guide necessary.

Sakli Kilise (The Hidden Church). This church, said to have been found only in 1963–4, is unfortunately much damaged and defaced. Situated close to the village of *Cemil*. Another church, provisionally known as the *Cemil Kilise*, is said to have been discovered close by, in 1965–6, but I found no trace of it.

There exists another church at *Gömede* known as the *Kara Kilise*, but I was unfortunately unable to visit it. Another church, known as the *Miriam Ana*, has also been named and adds confusion because there is already one church of the same name in the region. There is, finally, the monastery of *Archengolos*, consisting principally of a main refectory divided into two naves, and otherwise a mere series of arcades. It is older than the better-known monasteries in the village of Sinassos itself.

AT KARLI

The Church of St Eustace. Noted for its triple apse. Lies apart from the main community centres, but is probably just as old, going back to the ninth or tenth centuries. Some paintings survive. Another church, supposedly to St Theodore, is also said to exist in the same area, but I could not find it.

MISCELLANEOUS CHURCHES

Unimportant rock cell communities, none of which have any paintings at all, also exist at *Çat,* near Gülşehir, at *Arapli* on the Niğde to Kayseri road, and on the road to *Hacibektaş.* Cells of possible interest can be found at *Göre* on the outskirts of Nevşehir when going to Niğde, and at Ö*zkönak*, north of Avanos. The village of *Boğça,* though with rock cells, is too far off any decent road to be worth visiting. Some church cells also exist on the slopes of Hasan Daği.

A SHORT NOTE ON GUIDES

Very few sites can be found without the help of people who know the area very well: most churches are too well hidden to be found by amateurs. The following list of helpful people may therefore be of some use:

Guides for Göreme can be found at the ticket office on the site, but particularly helpful people whom one would do well to seek out include *Tahir Köse* or *Murat Köse*, *Hasan Kiran*, *Bayram Boylu*, and *Mustafa Torun*, all villagers in Ortahisar. The guide for the underground city at Kaymakli is *Mustafa Ağar*, who is very pleasant and, like the above, knows some English and a little French. The guide at Eski Gümüş is called *Mustafa Bayhan*, and at Soğanli ask for *Ziye Içli*, who lives in a cottage on the main road, and *not*, as far as can be ascertained, in the village of Soğanli itself. The guide for Sinassos is *Hayrattin Korkmaz*—the official man unfortunately, for he is rather mercenary and not very informative. If trying to find Özkönak, look for a dolmuş driver called *Şaban Bişgin* in Avanos, or go into the village of Özkönak and ask for either *Erol Kadir* or *Ali Özkan Bilha*.

Index

Index